UNIVERSITY OF ST. THOMAS LIBRARIES

WITHDRAWN
UST
Libraries

The Late Candidate

Also by Mike Phillips

BLOOD RIGHTS

The Late Candidate

MIKE PHILLIPS

St. Martin's Press
New York

THE LATE CANDIDATE. Copyright © 1990 by Mike Phillips. All rights reserved. Printed in the United States of America. No part of this book may be used or reproduced in any manner whatsoever without written permission except in the case of brief quotations embodied in critical articles or reviews. For information, address St. Martin's Press, 175 Fifth Avenue, New York, N.Y. 10010.

Library of Congress Cataloging-in-Publication Data

Phillips, Mike.
    The late candidate / by Mike Phillips.
       p. cm.
      ISBN 0-312-04866-1
    I. Title.
    PR6066.H485L38   1990
    813'.54—dc20   90-37256
                                                                                                                 CIP

First published in Great Britain by Michael Joseph Ltd.

First U.S. Edition: December 1990
10   9   8   7   6   5   4   3   2   1

This book is for Leila, Ivor, Esme, Baba, Rose, Trevor, Junior and me — together always; for Isisara, and for all the lost boys and girls from Shell Road, Kitty, wherever they are

My grateful thanks to Steve, to Kwesi, to JB and to RB, of course

The Late Candidate

Chapter 1

The call came at five in the morning.

I'd woken up from a dream that disturbed me, and I'd got out of bed and walked into the front room to watch the late night Dracula. After it ended Phil Donahue came on. The programme was about psychic phenomena, ghosts, flying saucers and all that stuff, and I watched in a daze, still thinking about my dream.

I was a child again, and I'd been alone with my mother in the house where we used to live in North London. I was locking and bolting the doors against some invisible threat, but my mother kept on saying, 'Where are they?' I knew she was talking about the rest of the family, but I couldn't answer her question.

I had come out of it struggling and shouting, and now, sitting in front of the TV, I was trying to make sense of the fading images when the phone rang.

I sat up, startled, because the sound, breaking the dead quiet of the early morning, was like a continuation of the dream.

It had to be, I thought, either a wrong number or my brother in New Jersey. He always rang me like this, late at night, when he got in at the end of the evening, dragging me out of bed at five or six. But I was always pleased when he called, and I picked up the phone planning to tell him that I was glad to hear his voice.

'Is that Sammy?'

It was a woman, and for a moment I didn't answer, poised halfway between disappointment and surprise.

'Is that Sammy Dean?'

This had to be trouble, and it was a black woman's voice, speaking with an inflection shaped by the dialect of the country where I had been born. I could guess what kind of trouble it was.

'Who's this?'

'Is it Sammy?'

'Yes, it's Sammy.'

'This is Eva, Eva Waite.'

For a moment I froze with shock. Eva was an old friend of my mother's, and the last time I'd seen her would have been nearly twenty years ago, in the house I'd been dreaming about.

'Eva,' I said, 'long long time.'

'It's been a long time, but I been keeping up with you.'

She'd followed my career, she said, and she'd seen me on telly not too long ago reporting on something or the other.

I grunted, remembering the occasion. I'd been dragged in for a quick burst of punditry about black businessmen, a subject on which I'd once written an article. The fee had been tiny and they'd taken a long time to pay it. For a poverty stricken freelance it wasn't a good memory.

'Eva,' I said, cutting her short. 'What can I do for you?'

'It's Tony,' she said, with a catch in her voice. 'They came and arrested him.'

My mind wandered. I must still have been half asleep because the words seemed to echo round and round my skull. Substitute another name and I was willing to bet I'd heard those words hundreds of times before, in exactly the same circumstances.

'Tony?'

'Tony. My little son. They just came and bashed down the door and arrested him.'

I'd last seen Tony as a toddler with a mischievous face and bright eyes. By this time he must be nearly twenty, I guessed.

'What for?'

'Murder.'
That woke me up.
'Murder?'
'Yes. They said he killed your friend Aston.'
'Aston? Aston Edwards? He's dead?'
'Yes. It was on the news. Didn't you see it?'
'No.'
There was a sparkle of excitement in Eva's voice. I'd heard this hundreds of times too. Underneath grief, panic, sorrow, hysteria, there'd be this bright little core of pleasure at being involved with something on the news.
'Well. They found him yesterday. In his car.'
'What happened?'
'What happened? They don't know. It was just that he'd been stabbed, and they found him dead. When I heard it I said to Mama, "Oh my God, look how they killed poor Aston." I didn't know they would come and arrest Tony for it, and he don't know anything.'
'So how they came for him?'
It was best to interrupt. If I let her talk she'd tell me every detail between now and then and back to his baby years.
'That's what I'm telling you,' she said. Her voice rose and took on a shrill note. 'We don't know. They just came and said they had a warrant and took him away. Then they started searching. I don't know. We never had any trouble with police. I thought it would kill Mama.'
'All right,' I said. 'You must keep calm. To help him. Where is he now?'
'They have him. At the station. He's coming up in court today. Can you come? The lawyer said to ring up everybody who could speak for him.'
This was familiar too. I had been on the telly and my name had been in the newspapers. Perhaps the white people who held Tony captive would listen to me.
'All right,' I said. 'I'll come to the house this morning.'
I put the phone down with a feeling in which grief and regret struggled with annoyance. This would be a bad day.

I picked up the phone to ring Aston's mother, then I realised that the old lady had died long ago. It was too early to ring anyone else and I decided to go down to the stall near the tube station and buy a newspaper.

As I approached the main road a little group of girls waiting on the corner looked round hopefully and then turned away, losing interest when they saw me. Their average age must have been sixteen but they were already streetwise enough to spot a useless prospect.

Walking to the newsagent's I deliberately focused my thoughts on the loitering girls. One of them must have been about fifteen, only a few years older than my son. At least he was safe in bed. I made a mental note to ring him later on, and at the same time I wondered whether the parents of the children on the corner knew where they were and what they were doing.

None of this worked, because, whatever I was thinking, I still kept hearing Eva say that Aston was dead and, as if tuned to the rhythm of my footsteps, images of him kept slipping in and out of my mind.

We had been born on the same day in the same street of our small village, and we'd been together every day that I could remember for the first dozen years of our lives.

Later, when we met in London, we would marvel over the fact that, after all, many years and thousands of miles away, we had come to live in the same place.

Now it was all over.

The newspaper confirmed what Eva had told me. A small report on the second page said that Councillor Edwards, controversial chair of construction services in a North London borough, had been found dead of stab wounds. He'd been slumped in the front of his car and the time of death hadn't been established.

Above the report there was a smudgy photo of Aston. That was all.

Chapter 2

Eva lived in a small terraced house in a short street off a main road. The bell gave out a series of chimes when I pushed it, and the door opened before they died away.

'Sammy,' Eva shouted.

She hugged me tight. She was a big woman, and it was like being embraced by a bear dressed in pillows. She sobbed a little, and the tears ran down my neck. Against me I felt the pillows heaving.

I pulled myself away feeling as if I'd been caught out in a storm.

'Nice to see you, Eva.'

'I've been waiting for you,' she said. 'To go to the court.'

She was dressed, I could tell, for a special occasion, in a navy-blue suit with a pleated skirt, and a heavy gold chain glinting around her neck.

'You're looking good,' I said.

'And you're a man now. Just look at you.'

She pulled me close again, kissed me on the lips, then turned and led the way into the back room to the left of the stairs.

I followed her trying to remember how old she would be. She'd been a lot younger than my mother and I guessed she was now in her late fifties, but she looked as vigorous as she'd always been. She was wearing high heels and, as I followed her down the passage, her big behind moved with a lazy, sexy rhythm that belied her age.

It was a dark, comfortable looking room with a big dining table on which a sewing machine stood. Near the table was a sofa facing a huge TV set. Eva's mother sat on the sofa watching TV and she didn't look up when we came in. Through the open door at the end of the room I could see the kitchen.

'Mama,' Eva said. 'Look, Sammy.'

She looked up then, adjusted her glasses and glared at me. Eva was dark brown but her mother was a freckly reddish-yellow and her face had a collapsed wrinkled look. In between the creases her eyes shone like bright green beads.

'Hello, Granny,' I said.

As kids we called her Granny because the adults called her Mama.

'Sammy,' she said accusingly. 'I saw you on the TV talking nonsense.'

I smiled weakly and spread my hands.

'You come to help Tony?'

'Yes, Granny.'

She grunted.

'I warned him,' she said. 'I warned all of you about those white women. But you don't listen.'

'Mama,' Eva said in a warning voice.

The old lady grunted again and turned back to glare at the telly.

'Let's go,' Eva said.

A light drizzle had started up outside. We had to hustle getting into the car and I started up and drove off without bothering about directions.

It was a familiar route. Left to the main road, past the recreation ground where I used to play football after school. On the other side between the rec and the churchyard, there was a long alleyway where I used to go with my first serious girlfriend. Halfway down we'd stop and feel each other, and after a while we'd progressed to doing it standing up.

Sometimes there'd be trouble in the area, which usually meant a fight between two groups of boys, black against white, or a black man beaten up, and at times like these she would tremble with fear and tension as we walked home; and as we turned into the alley we'd look back carefully to check that no one was following.

Driving past the churchyard brought those times back to me clearly. For a moment I was back in the alley, with Jane clinging desperately to me, my hands fumbling with the tiny packet, and reaching for the smooth warmth of her thighs above the stocking tops. All the time part of my mind listened intently for sudden noises or footsteps.

I looked past Eva remembering the blinding intensity of those encounters, and craning my neck to see up the alley.

She smiled as if she'd read my mind.

'You haven't been this side for a long time, eh?'

I nodded.

'You remember Jane?'

'The white girl?'

I nodded again. That was what they'd always called her, and my going with her had been a constant source of terror to my mother. Every time I went out late she sat up waiting, expecting me to come back beaten up and injured.

'It was a long time ago.'

Eva didn't reply, but I could feel her watching me intently.

When we got round the corner into the main road I picked out the court building immediately by the small crowd hanging around in front of it. On one side of the entrance there was a little group, mostly young, mostly black. On the other side was another group, of photographers, flanked by the sort of passers-by who had the time to spare for seeing the sights.

Eva went through them staring straight ahead, and I followed as close behind her as I could.

Inside, the corridors were crowded with people in black robes and white collars, all bustling back and forth purposefully. Some of them looked young, barely into their twenties, but even so they made me feel small and guilty in the way that lawyers seem trained to do.

Tony's solicitor, a slim middle-aged white woman with greying hair and a tight smooth face, showed us where to sit, and they brought Tony in before we'd quite settled ourselves.

He was a surprise.

Somehow I'd been half expecting someone a bit wild looking, perhaps with dreadlocks and a tough manner. In fact Tony looked like my idea of a college boy. He was tall and slender with broad shoulders, and he wore gold rimmed specs which gave him an elegant and slightly aloof air. It was easy to imagine him in a library or lining up at an athletics track.

While I studied Tony the lawyers began speaking in those droning bored tones they keep for the courtroom. His eyes searched the courtroom and lighted on his mother. He gave her a slight smile and raised his eyebrows a little, greeting her.

I looked round and saw her smiling back at him with the same curve of the lips.

On the other side of Eva, two seats down, I spotted a familiar profile. Coarse straw coloured hair sticking out over a big blunt nose, a gleaming brown eye. Borelli.

I had been bracing myself all along against the possibility of being called as a character witness. I suppose I'd been expecting something like a trial, but by the time I'd looked around a few times and begun to get a sense of what the lawyers were discussing it was all over.

Tony had been remanded, and they began taking him down again. As the policeman took his elbow and turned him round, someone shouted behind me. I looked up to see a tall black girl, with intricately plaited hair, pointing and shouting. I nudged Eva but she didn't look round.

In any case the disturbance was over in an instant. The lawyers moved around. New people came pouring into the courtroom, and when I looked again, the shrieking woman had disappeared.

Tony's solicitor had led Eva outside and was now talking to her in the corridor. She had a serious urgent air, and Eva listened with her head bowed, nodding a little from time to time.

Beyond them I saw Borelli standing a few yards away, his

expression moody and abstracted. I walked up to him.

'Hey, Spaghetti,' I said.

He looked up with an angry frown on his face. Then he recognised me and he rolled his eyes in resignation. I grinned. Last time we'd met I'd been in custody and I hadn't dared use the old schoolboy nickname.

'Prick,' he said.

'All right,' I said. 'Detective Sergeant Spaghetti, is it?'

He shook his head and gave me an exasperated smile.

'Still bloody wrong.'

'They've demoted you,' I said. 'I'm sorry to hear that.'

He rolled his eyes again.

'Promoted, mate. You're addressing Detective Inspector Borelli, old son.'

I stuck my hand out and we shook.

'Congratulations, mate. At least the old school's had one success.'

I meant it, even though Borelli had been one of my playground enemies at first, and as we went into the fifth year we'd stopped speaking altogether. I thought he'd been a lout and a bully as a boy and I had an instinctive dislike of being on social terms with a policeman. But in spite of all that our meetings had a warm and nostalgic feel.

'Yes. Well,' he said, 'bugger the old school tie. What are you doing here?'

'I know the bloke. Tony Waite. You anything to do with it?'

'I'm in charge of the investigation. Are you reporting on it?'

His tone was guarded now.

'No,' I told him. 'I just know his mum, you know. That's all.'

'All right, Sammy,' he said. His manner had changed. He couldn't wait to get away from me. 'I'll see you around.'

He moved away, mooching down the corridor. Eva came up beside me.

'That's the man,' she said. 'He made them search the house and take away clothes and things from Tony's room.'

She sounded almost tearful and I wondered what the lawyer

had been saying. Or perhaps it was just the atmosphere of the place, the feel of impersonal and merciless power.

'Come on,' I said. 'Best I get you back home.'

I put my arm round her and we walked out into the drizzling grey morning.

At the foot of the steps the tall woman with the plaits who'd shouted in court was blocking our way. I made to move round her, but Eva stopped.

'Margaret,' she said.

'Hello, Mum,' the woman said.

I got it at last. This was Tony's older sister.

'You remember Margaret,' Eva said.

'Yes.'

In fact I remembered a little skinny girl in ankle socks, with wide eyes and a cheeky grin. I couldn't see anything of that little girl in Margaret.

I put my hand out, but she didn't take it. Her expression was angry and hostile. She was still thin, but nowadays her body had a taut wasted look, like a distance runner in training. At the same time she seemed nervous and unhealthy, as if her emotions were wearing her flesh away from inside.

'Who sent you?' she asked.

I looked at Eva, but she was gazing away into the distance. No help at all.

'Your mother rang me.'

'And you came,' she said in a sarcastically understanding tone, 'just to see if you could help.'

'That's why I came.'

'That's very good,' she said in the same tone of voice, 'but who are you writing this up for?'

'I'm not, I just came because Eva rang me.'

Her expression didn't change.

'We're not stupid,' she said. 'You make your living writing about people. But we're not giving you any information to put in the papers. You hear that?'

She shifted her gaze to Eva.

'Tell him, Mum.'

Eva looked at me, and her expression was troubled and uncertain.

'I only came because you asked me to,' I told her firmly. 'If you want I'll go away again. It's up to you.'

Eva smiled at me. Then she gave Margaret a stern mother's look.

'Stop this nonsense, Margaret. I sent for Sammy and he's only here to help Tony. So just stop it.'

Margaret glared at me, but she shut up.

Back in the car the atmosphere was still tense and uncomfortable. I had hoped to be on my own with Eva, but Margaret had marched herself firmly into the back seat and I could feel her eyes burning into the back of my neck.

'What's the evidence against Tony?' I asked Eva.

'Didn't your police friend tell you?' Margaret said triumphantly.

'Stop it, Margaret,' Eva said, but her tone was perfunctory.

'That's a guy I knew at school. We don't meet too often, but I've got no reason to pass him on the street.'

'You've got no reason.'

Margaret laid the emphasis on the you. She was beginning to get right up my nose, but I was trying to stay cool for Eva's sake.

There was a short silence before Eva replied.

She said the police had found out about a confrontation between Aston and Tony on the day Aston died. Tony had been in Aston's house and Aston had dragged him out, slapped him around and thrown him into the street.

The boy had been out several hours that evening, and he'd come in about nine and gone to his room without greeting her or Granny. His story was that he'd been to a pub and a cinema, but he hadn't seen or spoken to anyone who knew him. Finally, the police had found a blood-stained shirt in his room. He said he'd had a nose bleed as a result of the fight, but no one could confirm that.

'Did Tony tell you about the fight?'

She shook her head.

'No. You know how young boys are. Sometimes he used to go for days without saying anything. He would just come in, say hello, and go to his room.'

'Mum,' Margaret said. 'If you're telling him, tell him the real thing. Tell him why Aston really slapped up Tony.'

'I don't know what you're talking about,' Eva said.

'Aston's wife,' Margaret burst out. 'Tony was in the house with her, that must be why Aston acted like that. She was always encouraging Tony. Everybody knew that. These bitches love to have two black men fighting over them. That's the only reason they arrested him.'

'I don't know anything about that,' Eva said. 'She was helping him with his studies.'

Margaret snorted derisively from the back seat.

'They always say they're helping.'

'I told him,' Eva said. 'It didn't look good. People like to talk and scandalize. Too much. Too much.'

'I'm not scandalizing,' Margaret said. 'But if you want to know who killed Aston, go and ask his wife. She was bound to have other men the way she carries on. But Tony's the scapegoat. You just ask her.'

She seemed to be working herself into a state of hysteria, but then she stopped.

When I looked at her in the mirror she had slumped against the window and was looking out. I glanced at Eva, but she had turned away from me and was gazing out of the other window.

I had lots of questions but I didn't want to hear any more of this litany of accusation against Aston's wife, and I had a hunch that if I started the conversation again that was how it would turn out.

Besides, Margaret had started me thinking about how I would approach the story if I had been writing it, and as I drove I began turning it over in my mind.

The rain had got heavier, slanting down in sheets, and I put the windscreen wipers on at full speed. Their clicking rhythm was the only sound to break the uneasy silence in the car, and we rolled down to Eva's house without speaking, each of us wrapped in our own thoughts.

Chapter 3

The rain had eased off by the time I turned out of the Edgware Road, but the streets were wet and miserable. I parked in front of the flat, hurrying a little as I anticipated getting inside and shutting myself off from the damp grey fabric of the city.

As I put the key in the lock I was fantasising about having a cup of coffee, putting my feet up, then dozing off in front of the telly for the afternoon, and I heard someone call my name two or three times before I responded.

I looked round and saw a short man in a respectable grey suit. He was light skinned, with a head of shiny black curls, and I recognised him with a definite feeling of irritation. *Walter Davis.*

'Walter,' I greeted him. 'What are you doing here?'

I hoped that I sounded fairly unenthusiastic. It wasn't that I didn't like Walter very much, although I didn't. The problem was that I knew he would ruin the rest of my day. I could feel it in my bones.

'I have to talk to you, Sammy. Let's go upstairs.'

Straight to the point. I sighed, then motioned him up the stairs ahead of me. The only bright spot was climbing up the three steep flights and seeing him falter in front of me as we neared the top.

When I pushed past him on the tiny landing to open the

door of my flat he was breathing heavily, almost panting.

'You're out of condition, son,' I said, smiling at him.

It was true. He had a slight paunch that he must have developed during the five years or so since I'd last seen him. Apart from that he looked the same. No reason why not, I thought. He wasn't thirty yet.

He made straight for my one armchair and sat down heavily.

'What can I do for you?' I said.

'I came to ask you to do us a favour.'

I knew the look on his face. The first time he'd walked into the office of the little magazine I used to edit he'd given me the same look, an acute balance of bullying and entreaty.

He'd been in his early twenties, just arrived in London after getting out of university in the little Welsh town where he'd spent all his life. He wanted to be a success, and he wanted for some reason to cut a figure in the black community.

He'd been brought up by a white couple who'd adopted him, and I think he must have spent a lot of his boyhood reading about famous black men like Martin Luther King and wanting to be like them.

I had introduced him to people and told him about London, helped him find a job, and listened to his problems. I didn't know why, except that he'd kept on asking me for help.

Now I thought about it, that was the sum total of our relationship and when he thought he didn't need me any more he'd drifted away.

I turned my back on him and looked out of the window at the rain dripping on to the pigeon droppings on the ledge.

'What's the favour?'

'It's not for me,' he said. 'It's about Aston.'

I should have known. Walter had become one of the spokesmen of the Labour Party black sections movement, and Aston had been one of their stars. He was also the chief press officer for the borough council on which Aston served. If there was a storm he'd be right in the middle of it.

'No one can do a damn thing for Aston now,' I said.

'There's more to it than that. You've got to understand what's happening. We knew as soon as we heard that they'd lay it on somebody black and they're going to use that to divide the whole movement.'

'Wait a minute,' I said. 'What are you on about?'

He drew his breath in sharply, made an angry gesture with his hands and gave me an impatient look.

'It's no use getting pissed off with me, son,' I said. 'I'm not one of your gang, so if you want me to help just tell me the whole story so I can understand what you're on about.'

He waggled his head.

'I told them you didn't understand politics.'

I came away from the window and moved towards him. Walter was one of those activists who took disagreement as evidence that you were either evil or stupid. But I was buggered if I'd put up with him patronising me in my own house.

'Listen, son,' I said. 'Don't jerk me around. You're not old enough or big enough for that, I know exactly who sent you.'

I named the two most influential members of the group I guessed had got together as soon as they'd heard of Aston's death.

'I was working with those guys in this town while you were still creeping round in Wales wondering what colour you were. Deliver the message or go back and tell them to come and see me. Either way is fine by me.'

'All right. All right.'

He laughed, shook his head and grinned at me. Intimidation hadn't worked, now he was going to turn on the charm.

'Don't get stroppy. You know I've got a lot of respect for your experience.'

'I'll take the respect for granted,' I said. 'Just tell me.'

He smiled sweetly, then put on a serious face.

'It's all about survival. Aston was just the first step.'

I kept my face straight. Political groups in a minority always put themselves at the centre of their universe, and every kind of event became part of a carefully orchestrated plot to do all of them down. Walter's case was different but at the bottom of it I knew there would be a sense of unrelenting persecution.

As I expected, he started by telling me that organised black groups on the left had always been under threat, but the real trouble had started when black members began organising within the Labour Party.

I interrupted him.

'I know all that, man. What's it got to do with this business?'

'You wanted to hear everything.'

I nodded.

'Okay. Well, you know the by-election's coming up this year.'

I'd forgotten that the sitting MP had died, but I nodded as if such matters were always on my mind.

'The militant left groups support us,' he said, 'because it annoys the leadership and it shows off their anti racism and they think they can use us when they want to. But they hate the idea that we've got different interests from the white working class and if they could, they would most certainly deny us a separate political identity.'

He paused. He felt in his pocket and took out a small packet of chewing gum, then he unwrapped it and put it in his mouth.

'The selection's going on now. You know what happens? It's a new system that's supposed to be more democratic. It gives every member a vote and it gives the trade unions voting rights too.'

'Make it short, man.'

'Each branch votes for its own short list. Then the names go forward to a meeting of all the branches where everyone votes for an overall short list. Then there's what they call an electoral college which includes the trade unions. So at that point they count up the votes from the members and the votes from the affiliated trade unions, and the person with the most points wins. The whole thing takes a couple of months, and the first branches are just about to start voting.'

'Democracy's confusing.'

'Well, only a few boroughs have operated it so far and no one's too sure how it works. But it's obvious you've got to have both the members' votes and the union votes if you want to be sure of winning. A lot of branches had Aston at the top of their lists, because he was well known and had a good record. The unions knew him too and he would have got their vote. Whoever gets it now will need solid backing from the local unions and a lot of friends among the members. Even if the bastards would vote for another black person it's too late to run a campaign.'

'Is that it?' I said. 'Are you trying to tell me that someone knocked him off to nobble the selection?'

'Not exactly. But you must realise that Aston was important locally, and he was going to be important nationally. We got a hell of a lot through the council because he had influence with those people and he knew how to make the system work for him.'

I nodded at him again. Aston was famous for pushing grants and payments through the town hall bureaucracy in half the time it would normally take. The local black groups would have lots of good practical reasons for missing him.

Walter must have misinterpreted my moody look.

'It's no bullshit,' he said urgently. 'Aston was really going to be big. He was brilliant. You know that. He was about the only one of us with grassroots trade union experience, and he was acceptable to a lot of people. The Cypriots, the Asians, the white liberals. I don't mean they loved him or anything like that, but he could talk to them and get them to do things his way.'

I turned to look out of the window, but I wasn't seeing anything. His words had put me in mind of how I'd run into Aston after all those years.

I'd been working at a factory in London during my summer vacation. There was another young black man on the next bench, and we'd smiled at each other, but it wasn't until the end of the day that I'd heard someone call his name and, hearing him speak, I'd known who he was.

Our reunion was joyous, the way it always was with one of the long lost homeboys, and Aston was a student on vacation too. But I soon found out that he already had serious political commitments.

When the factory went on strike, he was one of the organisers. The summer break ended, though, before the strike did, and I went back to college with a feeling of relief. Aston stayed, because, he said, leaving would be like giving up.

The next time I saw him, he was a minor union official.

Outside the window, a couple of pigeons landed and began to peck at the bread I'd put out for them. It was nearly all gone and I thought that it was time I gave them some more. But it was the kind of thing lonely old people did, and for a moment I envied Aston. Even as a dead man he mattered to people.

We'd gone in different directions over the last fifteen years, but all I could remember now was his energy and optimism during the strike. Bawling on the picket line or arguing with the other men at meetings, pressed by anger and trouble, he'd been happy.

'The first thing they did,' Walter said, 'was to pick up a black youth. That's how they work. If they can convict him, it will discredit us and demoralise the black community.'

'Any chance the youth is guilty?'

'I don't know,' Walter said. 'He's a college boy who used to hang around Aston. There's more chance that he's not guilty. I mean they could have picked up any number of people. You don't get that far in politics without making a few enemies. Know what I mean?'

'I know what you mean.'

'Besides,' Walter said irritably, 'there's more to it. I think they picked on this youth deliberately, because of the personal element. If they bring him to court they can rake up anything they like to try and smear Aston.'

'What could they rake up?'

'How would I know? You know these newspapers. Anything he did might get on the front page. What they'll try and do is make it into a brawl between two black men, drag his name down. They'll say the voters took this black man seriously and all the time he was up to no good. They're all the same. That's what they'll say.'

'What does Suzanne say?'

'Suzanne?'

Walter looked astonished, as if he'd never heard the name.

'Suzanne. Aston's wife. That's what it's all about, isn't it?'

Walter's expression got thoughtful and sincere. His voice took on a measured tone.

'Suzanne used to teach the boy. She encouraged him with his studies. The rumours were just the sort of smear they were always throwing at Aston. She made enemies too. When she got the job as the education deputy there was a lot of flak because she was Aston's wife. Influence. White woman. Black man. You know the kind of thing.'

'Who does she think did it?'

'Not Tony. She says he wasn't that sort. She thinks he couldn't have done it.'

'Okay, Walter. What do you want me to do?'

He hesitated.

'You were in court this morning. But you were gone before anybody could contact you. What's your interest? Are you writing about it?'

'Nope. I know the family. The mother rang and asked me to come.'

'So why don't you write about it?'

'Can't. Not at this stage. You know that.'

'Maybe not about the actual case. But you could write about Aston and write a bit about the politics he was engaged in. There can't be anybody better than you for it.'

'Maybe. It sounds like a good idea. I'll think about it.'

It probably was a good idea, and had it been someone else I'd have been on the phone trying to raise a commission. But somehow I felt squeamish at the thought of writing about Aston. In any case, many of the things I wrote came back to haunt me. As a freelance I had no control over the way things were edited or presented. Most of the time I didn't care, but whenever I wrote anything about the black community things were almost inevitably changed or put in a framework that caused deadly offence.

It didn't help to tell people that the white subs and editors couldn't think outside of racist categories or simply didn't know what they were doing. 'You lie down with dogs,' one of my friends once said bitterly, 'you get up with fleas.' Sometimes I went around for days with a naked vulnerable feeling, waiting for the next explosion of anger, and the thought of writing something about Aston and delivering it up to the sausage machine made me feel queasy.

Walter spotted my hesitation.

'I know you,' he said. 'You're only saying that to get rid of me. But you don't understand what we want you to do.'

His sharpness made me laugh.

'It's a couple of things really. If you can do just one piece with the political angle and concentrating on what a loss Aston is, other people will latch on to that. You know what the press are like. It's like sheep. One guy says something and they'll all go chasing that angle. If we can get a few decent stories, it will help.'

That made sense.

'What else?'

'If you're looking around you can find out things. You can talk to the police. Since the police committee took them on they won't talk to us. It would be worth knowing what they've got. The more we know the more we can pressure them to get after the real villains. And the town hall. There's a lot of people there who'll be celebrating. Aston was after something. He'd got some information down in housing that he was sorting out last week. There's some big crooks in there and he was trying to shake them out.'

'In the town hall?'

'Of course in the town hall. You think politics is some joke?'

I stared at him, trying not to look excited. Walter knew very well that a tale of buried secrets and corruption would hook me, but I didn't want to give him the satisfaction of thinking he was pulling my strings.

The other problem was that if the whole affair was a simple crime of passion, Walter and his friends would still want to create as much confusion as possible, and they'd want to use me to spread suspicion.

I shrugged. There were too many angles to sort out now. But I owed something to Aston's memory. I didn't know what it was, but I did know that now I'd been invited in I couldn't keep out.

'I'll give it a go,' I told Walter.

Chapter 4

Suzanne rang me during the evening. Her voice sounded hoarse and spongy as if there was something wrong with her throat.

'Sammy,' she said, without preliminaries. 'You heard about Aston?'

'Yes, I'm sorry.'

'The funeral's in a few days. I know he would have wanted you to be there. You have to be.'

'Yes.'

Suddenly I had the sense that she was about to put the phone down. She'd said what she had to say.

'Suzie, I know you're having a hard time, but I need to speak to you.'

She said nothing for a little while. There was a buzzing sound on the line, and I listened to it, wondering what she was thinking.

'Yes, you would,' she said eventually. 'Come to the house in the morning. I'm going back to Cambridge with my parents for a while, but I'll wait for you.'

I didn't sleep much that night. I didn't go to bed. Instead I sat up watching TV and dozing fitfully. In between I thought about Aston and Suzie.

They always say that it's the unpredictable which makes life exciting. The problem is that once you've been around long enough to see the same things happening over and over again, the bad bits aren't unpredictable any more. You know anything could happen, but you keep your fingers crossed.

When I introduced Aston to Suzie it didn't occur to me that any consequences would follow. I remembered the occasion well, because it was the day that Suzie and I had got our exam results, and we were in a coffee shop with some other people when Aston walked in.

I'd been going out with Suzie from time to time. It was a loose arrangement, and it didn't surprise me when they went off together. But there were some lubricious grins round the table.

'She's at it again,' someone muttered, and a couple of people sniggered.

It might just have been the silly sort of piss taking comment one person or the other had been making all morning, but in that moment, the atmosphere had changed, and there was real malice to the remark.

Our campus was renowned as one of the most radical in the country. We were famous for our demos, and hate figures like Enoch Powell could transform the institution into a seething arena of political passion.

On the other hand, the same students thought that going out with a black factory worker was a kind of sexual aberration.

In the fifteen years or so since that day she'd lost touch with most of the people who'd been in our class then; except for me, and I wasn't looking forward to our next meeting.

Thinking about the funeral I shivered. Through the curtains I could see the sky getting lighter in preparation for the grey morning. I hadn't noticed the rain, but the pavements outside were wet and glistening. I could tell it was going to be another damp, dirty day.

It was raining when I drove through Camden Town, and the water streamed down the windscreen in thick mournful dribbles like the tears of an ugly giant.

The traffic moved slowly, even though it was nearly halfway

through the morning, and well past the rush hour. But I didn't mind. The slow crawl put off the encounter with Suzie and gave me time to think.

I'd have to ask her about the rumours which linked her to Tony. They could be defused by circulating a sanitized version of the truth. But unless Suzie had changed a lot it would be a ticklish business.

I was still wrestling with the problem as I went past Wood Green, but the sky was getting lighter and, as if in response, the traffic had thinned out. In no time at all I was turning into the crescent where Aston had lived.

It had the sort of countrified charm that was typical of the suburban end of the borough. The houses, built in the early twenties, were detached from each other, with gardens sloping down to the pavement, and along the street a row of silver birches broke up the outline, giving it a leafy peaceful air.

I parked in front of Aston's house and by the time I was walking up the path Suzie had the door open.

I had seen her several times since we'd been classmates but now I found myself looking carefully at her, trying to see her as other people did.

She was still blonde, with grey eyes which seemed to have changed colour every time you looked. She wore a black dress which fitted tightly round the bust and hips, and when she moved I saw that the skirt had a slit which showed off her long slim legs.

She looked good. Perhaps better than she did when I first met her. The years had given her a fuller, softer silhouette and added warmth and humour to her face. But some things hadn't changed.

It was typical, I thought, that even dressed as a widow Suzanne looked sexy.

I went up to her and without words we put our arms around each other. Then her body seemed to heave like a pump starting, and she was sobbing uninhibitedly, like a child.

We stood like that in the doorway for nearly a minute, and then I eased her into the hall, and closed the door behind me.

She didn't let go but I kept her moving, into the big room which ran the length of the house. There was a sofa near the door and I put her on it.

She loosed her grip on me then and lay back with her hands covering her face.

'I'm sorry,' she said, between sobs and without removing her hands.

'Come on kid,' I told her. 'Cry all you want.'

But she didn't. As soon as I'd said that she seemed to stop crying. From behind her hands she looked at me, raised her eyebrows and shrugged ruefully. Then she swung her legs down, and got up. She kept her face turned away from me as she spoke.

'Sorry, Sammy. Give me a minute.'

Without pausing she hurried out of the door we'd come in and I heard her clattering up the stairs.

Left to myself I looked around. The room was big and comfortable. Two sofas, a leather armchair, a rocking chair and a small dining table with books and papers scattered over it. Against the wall a bank of shiny video and stereo equipment. At the far end a sort of glassed-in patio which looked out on to a large garden. In the middle were a couple of pear trees with a carpet of rotting fruit lying around them.

Aston had done all right, I thought. But none of this would do him any good now.

Opposite me was an antique cupboard and I went over to it, knowing what I would find. Right first time. It was full of bottles. The brandy was at the back and I hauled out a fat one with a definite feeling of satisfaction.

Suzie came back just as I was getting it open. She sat down without comment and I filled a glass and handed it to her. That was my one piece of unambiguous medical knowledge. In situations like this people drank brandy.

'What did you want to know?' she asked. Her face was still flushed and her eyes were red, but she was back in control.

'Everything that happened to Aston.'

She frowned.

'I'll tell you what I know.'

I nodded and she sat up in her seat, her hands clasped in her lap. For some reason I could hardly look at her, and I stared out at the garden while she talked.

She'd been waiting at home for Aston to arrive. They'd been due to go out to the opening of the new youth centre. She hadn't worried at first because he was often held up by one thing or another. But later on she'd started ringing people. No one had seen him since about lunchtime. Eventually when the doorbell rang she'd gone rushing out thinking that perhaps he'd forgotten his keys, but it was the police. Detective Inspector Borelli.

She paused for a moment and I thought she was going to start crying again but she didn't. She lifted her chin and stared past me at the wall.

'They told me Aston had been found dead in his car. After that I don't know. I sort of collapsed. My parents arrived a few hours later and found me crawling around the floor howling. They drove all the way down in a few hours, poor souls. They've been looking after everything?'

'What about the police? Did they ask you anything?'

She took her gaze off the wall then and looked at me. I couldn't read her expression but something had happened behind her eyes.

'They came back yesterday and asked me a lot of questions. About our friends. Whether I knew where he was that night. That kind of thing. The car was parked near the youth centre. But I was absolutely certain that he'd meant to come home and pick me up before we went there. They seemed to think that was suspicious.'

'Anything else?'

She frowned, her eyes narrowing into slits and glinting dangerously.

'You're beginning to sound like them,' she said. 'What's all this for, Sammy?'

I should have seen it coming. She used to lose her temper easily and I could recognise the signs. There were three parallel lines across her forehead and her jaws were clenched tight. She had no idea, I used to tell her all those years ago, how intimidating she could look. But now, seeing the familiar signs of anger on her face, I felt a rush of nostalgic affection, as if I had just remembered something nice we'd done together.

I'd been about to answer, but instead I just looked at her, letting her see that I shared her misery.

She hid her face behind her hands again. Then took them away.

'All right,' she said. 'They asked me about Tony. The boy they arrested.'

'What about him?'

'Someone told them that Aston had thrown him out of the house that day.'

She took her hands away from her face and leaned back, looking at the ceiling.

'That wasn't all of course. According to Mr Borelli. There were rumours.'

'So what was all that about then?'

She raised her head and looked at me.

'He's innocent you know. He didn't do it.'

'Why have they arrested him?'

She took a tissue from the box beside her, blew her nose, wiped her face and leaned back again.

'They arrested him because they think we were screwing and Aston came in and caught us at it.'

'Is that what they said?'

'No. It's what they thought. Borelli could hardly contain himself.'

I could imagine. At school Borelli had reached puberty faster than most of us. That made him an adult, and for nearly a year he'd boasted about his prowess as a masturbator before the rest of us caught up. Sometimes there would be closed sessions in the third floor toilets, and Borelli, red faced and sweating with ecstasy, would demonstrate to a circle of admiring juniors.

'Well,' I said. 'If that's not it, what?'

Suzie sat up, leaned forward, dabbed her eyes and looked me

full in the face, her eyes worried and questioning.

'I need to know why you're asking, Sammy. What's going on?'

Without hesitating I told her about Eva's phone call, about going to the court and about Walter's visit. When she heard what Margaret had said her expression didn't change.

'I'm ready to believe the boy didn't do it,' I said. 'There are some boys who might do a thing like that but Tony didn't look the type. Besides, there's no way that Aston would let a boy like that hurt him.'

'Everybody knows that,' Suzie said. 'Except the police.'

'If they're wrong about the motive they won't get very far.'

I didn't know if I believed that, but it seemed the right thing to say.

She leaned closer and took my hands between hers.

'It's more complicated than that,' she said. 'I know Tony didn't do it, but if you're going to help you must try and understand what was happening.'

'I'm still your friend,' I said.

Chapter 5

She stared at me for a moment then she seemed to make up her mind.

'It's a long story and it's all about Aston and me really. You know what he was like. I suppose I was so conceited about my own looks that it didn't strike me that he'd fancy anyone else. Not for a long time anyway. But after a couple of years I realised something was going on. This woman kept ringing up. I remember she rang up just before we went away on holiday and we had a row about it. I nearly didn't go. Just as well I did. He told me all about it sitting on a balcony in Barbados looking out over the sea. We sat there all night talking and the next night and the next. It was crazy. We were shouting at each other. Eventually I kind of understood.'

She grinned. Talking about those days seemed to take her mind off and make her more animated. I nodded encouragingly.

'Of course I wouldn't have been at all understanding if he'd been white but I knew his attitude to sex and all that was different. Or I just wanted to believe what he said about cultural differences and all the rest of it. And he had a way of convincing you somehow that he deserved it. I don't know. He worked so hard. He was under so much pressure. I knew that so well. He was special. Sometimes I felt sort of churlish having a go at him.'

She paused, thinking about it.

'I suppose I also thought it was a one-off and he wouldn't do it again. When we came back she rang up and I told her I knew all about it. I felt quite triumphant. I didn't realise that for Aston it was a very handy way of getting rid of her. He was probably on to someone else by then.'

I smiled. We used to meet more frequently during that period and Aston used to talk about the women he met as if he were a bachelor. But it was also true that where we came from that didn't mean that he was indifferent to his wife or careless about his marriage. In his book it was just the sort of thing that men did.

'People who knew he screwed around thought I must have been in a state about it. But I wasn't. Not really. Sometimes it hurt a bit, but after a while I realised that he didn't give them anything. Not a lot of affection. Not even time. And I still loved him desperately. We still had a good time together. All that. I thought we'd have kids any minute and everything would change.'

She got up and walked a few paces towards the window. She stayed there, standing with her back to me.

'It's funny. Things did change, but that was when I realised that I couldn't have children. Chicken and egg I suppose, but at the same time the political thing began to happen for Aston. He started working for the union. He loved it. I got my first serious job in education. It was absorbing. We were away from each other a lot. I started screwing around too.'

She came back towards me, picked up the brandy bottle, poured me one and took her glass away to the table, where she sat, her face still turned away from me. I waited. Sometime during the conversation the rain had started coming down heavily again. We watched it together in silence for nearly a minute, then she turned round and looked at me.

'He knew of course. I told him after the first time. I don't know what I expected, but he was moody for a little while, then I had the impression he was sort of relieved. It was funny, everything went on the same as before. We just didn't talk about it. Not much anyway. The thing he hated was gossip. I had to be very discreet. That wasn't hard. Being a married woman gives you a lot of protection. The rule is to misbehave yourself away from home. Abroad. In another town. Make the limits very clear. Be firm. That kind of thing.'

I got up, went over to the table and sat opposite her. She faced me now with her chin resting on her hands.

'So. It went on like that for years till I got bored and stopped. Well, it wasn't a big decision. It was just that one year I noted that I hadn't done anything like that for a while. Then there was all the business about AIDS. We talked about that and we agreed. No chances.'

She poured another brandy out. Her hand shook a little. She started talking again, faster, a little impatiently as if she wanted to get it all out and be done with it.

Tony had been her protégé. He'd messed up his school exams then joined her college so he could do them again. He was a bright, hard-working sixteen-year-old, and teaching him was a pleasure. It was as if he was waking up for the first time. She gave him books. They talked about them. He came around to the house and borrowed more. He helped in the garden. She taught him chess. He admired Aston and Aston talked to him a lot, told him about politics and what was going on in the borough.

Imperceptibly he became part of their lives.

She closed her eyes and moaned. Then she looked at me again and carried on talking as if nothing had happened.

'I used to have these fantasies about adopting him. I don't know. Maternal instincts. Then one day about six months ago, it would have been about three years after he started coming around, I noticed that he was growing up. He rang to ask me about something and his voice sounded like a strange man's for a moment. I made a joke about it. It happened a short time after that. A very short time.'

She lifted her glass and drained it.

'What happened?'

'What do you think? Sex. The whole thing. I couldn't keep

my hands off him. Well. He was nineteen. He wasn't my pupil any more.'

She smiled.

'It was like being his mother and a twenty-year-old girl all at the same time. I told myself it was all right, but I couldn't tell Aston.'

'Why not?'

She gave me one of her direct looks.

'Well. I had all sorts of ways of justifying it to myself but it always felt a bit like incest. He'd become like part of the family.'

She stopped. I waited. She frowned at me.

'It's funny,' she said. 'I can't read your expressions any more. Are you shocked?'

I shook my head. Her story might have merited headlines in a Sunday tabloid, but I'd known a number of nice, respectable women in their thirties who'd had wilder experiences.

I told her so, and she nodded soberly.

'Anyway,' she said, 'Aston found out. Some bag in the town hall told him that everyone was gossiping about me and Tony. I think Tony must have told someone. Probably his wretched sister. Aston came home in a fury. I'd embarrassed him.'

She went on, hurrying again. He'd accused her. She'd accused him back. They'd shouted and screamed at each other half the night, then made it up, and by the morning she'd agreed to stop the affair. That was when the trouble started.

'He took it badly. He kept on calling up and coming round when I was on my own. I felt rotten about it, but I'd promised Aston. In the end I had to tell him. Tony was ringing up five, six times a day. I had to do something. So we decided to see him together. To explain. Aston thought if he talked to him ... So I called him up and asked him to come round. At lunchtime. I had the morning off and Aston came back early.'

'That was the other day.'

'Right. It wasn't a success.'

'What happened?'

'To begin with he didn't know Aston would be there, and when he realised what was happening he started shouting, almost hysterical. Whore. Whore. He kept shouting that at me.'

She leaned back and stared at the ceiling.

'What did you do?' I said hurriedly.

'Aston got in a rage. He grabbed him and hustled him out of the door. I heard him slapping him. Oh, two or three times. Then he closed the door and came back. We talked. He thought Tony would calm down in a little while. Then he went off to the town hall. He had some kind of appointment. That was the last time I saw him.'

She closed her eyes, screwing them up tight.

'There was one thing I didn't tell the police. Tony had a knife. He took it out when Aston grabbed him, and Aston took it away from him. I think that's why he slapped him.'

'What happened to it?'

'I don't know. Aston said he'd talk to him about it when he calmed down. He was going to tick him off for carrying it. He said it didn't mean anything. He took it out to the car, I think. He wouldn't have given it back to him.'

She opened her eyes and they were streaming with tears. She put her face in her hands and began to make a howling sound. I got up, walked round the table, put my arms around her and patted her gently on the back.

'All right, love,' I said over and over again.

I wanted to cry too, but I couldn't. Instead I stared out at the garden which seemed somehow to have gone dim, out of focus, and in a moment the rain, which had stopped for a little while, started coming down again.

Chapter 6

The police station was in the old High Street. I thought of it in that way even though three or four of the old boroughs had been amalgamated to form one giant administrative unit. There were now several High Streets, nearly all of them almost identical, each one complete with a town hall, a police station and a line-up of chain stores, flanked by shopping arcades and hamburger joints.

In twenty years the look of the buildings had changed and some of the names, but the basic patterns stayed the same. When I saw pictures of London in magazines or brochures I recognised the familiar landmarks like Big Ben, but they had little to do with the city I lived in. To me London was an endless succession of streets like this, their features continually altering and reforming, grimaces on the face of a toothless old man.

I parked opposite the station and went up the steps. They'd extended the building at the back, but kept the old red brick façade with its curving archway. Beyond it two policemen were sitting behind a counter.

One of them had greying hair, horn rimmed specs and a clipboard. I smiled at him.

'I'd like to speak to Inspector Borelli please.'

His face stayed blank. His eyes gave me a professional survey.

'Is he expecting you, sir?'

I didn't hesitate. If my reply was in any way ambiguous he'd think I was trying to complain or protest about something, and he might get rid of me without even telling Borelli I was there.

'Yes, he is. Tell him it's Sampson Dean,' I said.

He pursed his lips and picked up the phone.

'There's a gentleman here for Inspector Borelli. Says he's expected.'

He kept on looking at me.

'What's it all about, sir.'

I frowned and gave him my most serious expression.

'Inspector Borelli knows what it's about. Just tell him it's Sam Dean.'

He spoke into the phone again, then put it down.

'Would you like to wait. In there.'

He pointed to the waiting room on the left of the counter. I nodded, smiled and went in.

The room was bare and had an uncomfortable institutional look, like a railway waiting room.

On the bench opposite me was a little West Indian family, a fat woman with two small boys. They looked as if they'd been there a long time. From time to time the woman muttered under her breath, her eyes closing as if in prayer. I grinned and winked at the boys but their mother frowned and glared at me. It was obvious that she didn't want her kids communicating with the sort of man who found himself in police stations. I didn't blame her.

Through the glass I saw Borelli emerge from behind the counter and the police sergeant spoke to him and pointed in my direction. I gave him a little wave, but he turned and had a few more words with the other cops before coming towards me.

I got up in my turn and we met in the doorway of the waiting room.

'What do you want?'

His voice was aggressive and surly in exactly the way I remembered it. I struggled for a tone that wouldn't antagonise him.

'Well, Franco,' I said, 'I haven't seen you for a long time and I thought I would buy you a drink. To congratulate you.'

His eyebrows shot up. We hadn't ever been mates and he wasn't falling for that one.

'Besides,' I went on quickly. 'You're in charge of the Aston Edwards case and I thought we should talk. Maybe I can help you.'

'Help me?'

He looked sceptical. His mouth twisted in a sneer, then he seemed to think better of it, and something that would be a cunning leer when it grew up replaced it. It was depressingly easy to read what he was thinking because the expressions clicked across his face like the names on a railway timetable.

'What have you got in mind?'

Before I could reply two young black men came out of a door opposite, swaggered across and pushed past us. They were about the same age, and had identical haircuts, cropped close to the scalp with a pair of zigzag partings on each side. As they went they stared us in the eyes as if daring us to fight, and one of them made a sound in his throat, which could have been a word or an involuntary growl.

In the waiting room the fat woman rose to greet them, but I couldn't hear what they were saying because Borelli took my arm and drew me towards the street.

'Let's go next door and take that drink,' he said. 'Your shout.'

The pub next to the station was open, although the lunchtime drinkers had mostly gone, and it was dim and quiet.

We sat on two stools at the end of the bar, and Borelli ordered a pint of bitter, then when the drinks came, regarded my orange squash with good-natured contempt.

'What's your game then?'

This was the first move. I really wanted to know what he had on Tony, whether he had witnesses or any other suspects, whether they'd recovered the weapon, and most important, whether they'd decided to go after Suzie.

Some of it was stuff he'd be willing to tell any reporter, some of it wasn't, and those were precisely the bits I couldn't ask him about. It wasn't that they were deadly secrets he would die to preserve. Most crime reporters had their moles in the force who would tell them anything. The trouble was that the trade usually went both ways.

'I'm writing an article now, about Aston.'

I told him quickly about our friendship.

'I've got quite a lot to tell you about the background and I'm going to be looking about talking to people. I mean, a big-time detective like you, there's probably a lot you'll want to know that I can tell you. I don't know if you've solved the case but even if you have it might help.'

He frowned and fixed me with a suspicious glare.

'Get this straight, Sammy. If you find anything that's evidence I want to know. Otherwise I can get you for withholding it. Don't worry. I don't have to make any deals with you.'

Tony's knife flashed through my mind. I held up my hands in a placatory gesture.

'Franco,' I said. 'I know you're hard, mate. You don't have to prove it to me.'

'Bloody right.'

That was as ingratiating as I wanted to get, I thought. I smiled at him.

'Right,' I said. 'The thing is how are you going to know what I find out unless I feel like telling you? I mean I don't suppose you guys have developed a machine that can read minds.'

'I don't need a machine for that.'

The suspicious glare was still in place. This isn't working, I thought, but I had an inkling what the problem was. At school the only way to get the better of hard kids like Borelli was to use words. Putting him down in the classroom where he couldn't hit you had been easy. He'd grown up with a settled hostility to fast talkers, and now I knew he was wondering what trick I was about to pull on him.

I tried another tack.

'Franco, I need a favour. I'm writing this article and there's all kinds of details which didn't get into the papers or that I might have missed. I don't want to cock it up, so help me out. A little favour, man.'

His expression cleared up suddenly, as if he'd just remembered at last that he was grown up and in a position to patronise me, no matter how clever I thought I was.

'All right,' he said. 'Don't grovel. Get them in again and you can have ten minutes' conversation. Then I must be off. Can't hang around yakking with the likes of you.'

I signalled to the barman and Borelli smirked as if he'd put one over on me.

I asked him some of my questions and he replied with a carelessness that showed his mind was at rest.

Someone had stabbed Aston from in front with a long pointed knife. That seemed to indicate it was someone he knew or someone he was having a fight with. Then they'd put him in the car and driven it to the spot where it was found. A police car had patrolled past about half past eight and hadn't seen it. When the same patrol had come back an hour later they'd got out to take a look because the car was oddly parked with one wheel up on the pavement. Aston was slumped in the front seat and covered with blood.

'It's a bit funny, that no one around there saw anything.'

'You know what they're like,' Borelli said, 'but we'll find someone in the end.'

That meant there were no witnesses. But Borelli must have gone straight to Tony's house. The only reason for that must have been a tip-off from someone who'd given him good enough reasons for arresting the boy.

'I take it you got the tip about the youth you nicked over the phone. Was it a man or a woman? They must have told you about the fight and the blood on his shirt. Was it one of his mates?'

He didn't like this bit. He considered me moodily. He reached up and smoothed his fringe back.

'This is off the record,' he said. 'If I see this in print you're for it.'

'What?' I put on a shocked tone. 'What? I mean the biggest

idiot must be able to guess you were acting on information received.'

'That's it. Information received. Nothing about the telephone and the blood on his shirt. Nothing like that.'

'Sure,' I said. 'That's understood.' I went on quickly. 'The other thing I heard was that you were looking into the rumours. I guess you heard about them from the same source.'

'What rumours?'

He brushed his fringe back again. In the old days he used to rub his forehead nervously but he'd stopped that now.

'You know exactly what rumours, man. It's all over the place.'

'People make all kinds of accusations in a case like this. You must know that.'

He was suddenly being very cautious. I sensed that he would walk out in a moment.

'All right,' I said. 'But do me a favour. You've got no confession, no witnesses, no murder weapon. All you've got is a body, a tip-off and a suspect. Either you're working through a list of suspects or you're working on the motivation, 'cause a slap in the face isn't enough. Not with this kid. He's not the vicious type. You know that.'

Borelli's expression had turned stony and he didn't reply. Instead he lifted his glass and drained it.

'You've had your ten minutes,' he said. 'If I was you I'd be careful what I write. Know what I mean?'

He got up and walked out without another word, and I sat back for a moment thinking about the conversation.

The only useful thing I'd learnt was about the telephone tip Borelli had received, and it had to be important. If Tony's claim that he hadn't seen or spoken to anyone he knew that day was true, then it must have been Aston who'd told the informant about the fight and about Tony's relationship with Suzie.

The fact that he or she had chosen to pass it on anonymously could only mean that they'd killed him or had some reason for keeping their connection with him secret. At the least they would have seen Aston that evening and known something about what he was doing or where he was going.

It wasn't much, but it was the wrong note I'd been looking for, and it gave me a loose thread on which to tug. With any luck the puzzle would begin to unravel.

In any case the way things were shaping up it was important to find the person, whoever it was. It was possible that Borelli had his doubts about Tony's guilt, but police routine called for quick, clear solutions and unless he was presented with a much better bet very soon, all his efforts would be directed towards sending down the suspect he had his hands on.

Sooner or later he'd be able to establish what was going on between Suzie and the boy, and at that point anything could happen.

I got up and walked out of the pub. It had stopped raining for the moment, but the dirty grey sky seemed to be hanging lower and lower over the buildings, as if it meant to keep on moving inexorably downwards until it flattened the city.

I hurried along to the car, opened the door, got in quickly and started the engine. Safe at last.

Chapter 7

I spent most of the afternoon on the telephone, trying to find an editor who wanted me to write about Aston. When I found one, what she wanted was nice and simple, a straight piece of biography and a little speculation about what his death would mean to local politics.

As for how he died and why, she wasn't very interested.

'Leave that to the police,' she said.

I told her I would, put the phone down and rang Walter. He sounded grumpy and preoccupied, although he cheered up a bit when I told him I was going to write the article.

'Good. The tabloids and the local paper have been on my back for the last few days. God knows what those bastards are going to say.'

'It's not hard to guess,' I said.

He was silent for a moment.

'What can I do for you, Sammy?' he asked eventually. 'It's kind of busy around here.'

I thought over everything Suzanne had told me. If I left young Tony out of it, the only area that offered any clues was the youth centre.

He'd been on his way there and his body had been found nearby. More than likely someone had seen him and spoken to him or even had some inkling about who else he'd seen that night. Flimsy, but I had to try it.

'Where's the youth centre?'

'Why do you want to know?' Walter suddenly sounded guarded.

'That's the last place I can connect Aston to,' I said.

'All right, but I'd better go with you,' he said. 'They're fed up being questioned by police and hassled by reporters and you're a stranger. If you go up there on your own nobody will talk to you and if they suss you somebody might bash your face in.'

He chuckled, as if considering the prospect gave him a grim pleasure.

We arranged to meet later, and he said he'd fix a meeting with the manager of the centre.

After I put the phone down I sat down in front of the typewriter and tried to fool myself that I was going to write about Aston. But everything I typed seemed trivial or sentimental and in the end I gave it up and just sat there staring out of the window.

The sun had struggled out to watch over the dying day, and the pigeons were hopping around in its watery light.

The phone rang several times in the next couple of hours. At first I ignored it. I was in a mood to ignore everything, but eventually, just as the last bright gleams began fading from the sky behind the Post Office tower, I picked it up and said hello. It was my son.

'Where've you been, Dad?'

I told him about Aston and he was silent for a few seconds.

'I saw it on the news,' he said.

Another pause.

'Are you sad?'

'Yes.'

'Sorry Dad.'

'Okay.'

We talked a little while longer. He said he'd come and see me soon, then he said goodbye and put the phone down.

I went back to watching the sky feeling disturbed and angry.

My son had never seen the place where I was born. He wouldn't even be able to imagine me as a child, playing cricket in the middle of a village street with Aston.

The phone rang again. This time it was Sophie.

'You're back,' I said, my spirits lifting.

She'd been away for a few weeks taking photographs for a magazine feature and I told her quickly about Aston. She said she was coming round and I told her I'd be out till later.

'I'll come anyway,' she said. 'When you get back.'

That lifted the gloom a little and, for a while, as I went down the stairs, got in the car and set out to meet Walter, I felt incongruously light and cheerful.

Halfway there I found myself thinking about Suzie. What she'd told me gave Tony a strong motive, but I still couldn't imagine him as Aston's killer. He'd have run away, or come up with some sort of alibi. Besides, Suzie was sure that he hadn't done it and I trusted her instincts.

On the other hand, I thought, she had every reason in the world to persuade me of his innocence. Fifteen years ago I could have sworn that she wouldn't lie. Now I couldn't be sure.

Borelli's informant crossed my mind. It didn't prove anything, but it was some comfort out there on the edge of trust.

Preoccupied by thoughts like these I almost missed the spot where I'd arranged to meet Walter, and I would have if he hadn't been there, leaning against his car, gazing moodily across the street.

I pulled up, parked on the corner and got out. Around me the blocks that made up the huge housing estate towered like cliffs decorated with the long barred lines that represented the walkways. Familiar as they were I could never get used to the way the place looked, like a monstrous set in a fifties sci fi movie, and it wouldn't have surprised me much if alien beings in silver plastic suits had suddenly emerged from one of the buildings. The whole place had that kind of eerie feel. It was fairly early, about eight, but the place seemed silent and deserted, except for a small knot of black boys lounging halfway down the crescent.

I was facing Daley Thompson Crescent, where the youth centre was, and once out of the car I could hear a pounding bass line overlaid with braying synthesiser riffs. Music from outer space. I had the illusion that the area was vibrating with the sound.

As Walter came close to me he clicked his fingers and pointed.

'That's where they dumped him.'

Somehow I felt that there ought to be something memorable about the spot, but it was just a stretch of pavement.

'Let's go,' I said.

'Wait a minute.' He put his hand on my arm. 'What exactly are you up to?'

I told him I was trying to get a picture of what Aston had been doing and who he'd seen before he was killed.

'He was a busy man. His normal day was a list of one appointment after another. The gap between teatime and when they found him must be important. Either he was on the job or he was meeting someone who was giving him some kind of information or making some kind of deal they don't want made public. If we can establish that it creates a whole new range of possibilities for the cops to work on. At the moment they're concentrating on Tony and unless they get their teeth into something else you'll soon be reading every headline you ever had nightmares about.'

That aspect of it didn't bother me very much but I knew it would concentrate Walter's mind. It wouldn't take much to convince him that his enemies were closing in. I mentioned my conversation with Borelli and his expression grew anxious. He swore softly.

We'd been standing there a little while and I looked past him to check whether anyone was looking out at the street. There was a chance that someone peeking out might have seen Aston's car being parked. But all the lighted windows had their curtains firmly drawn.

It crossed my mind that Walter had more at stake than he'd let on. The scandal might hurt the local party, but I could hardly believe that would make him as anxious as he seemed.

45

'Aston was well known around here,' I said. 'Somebody might have seen him, seen his car. It's worth asking.'

Walter grunted absently. I took it for consent and we walked in unison round the corner.

I had imagined from the noise that the youth centre would be packed with people, but my first impression after we'd pushed through the swing doors was of a vast, shadowy and empty space. As my eyes began to adjust, I realised that it was merely the effect of the dim lighting coupled with the size of the place.

We had actually walked into a long room with a raised stage at one end, on which there was some sort of sound system blasting out the music. Blobs of coloured light flitted rapidly across the floor like giant phantom butterflies, but they had the odd effect of creating shadow, making it even more difficult to see the surroundings.

'Where's the crowd of happy, dancing youths?' I bellowed into Walter's ear.

'Nothing much happening tonight,' he shouted back.

I could see that for myself, but it still seemed strange, considering the history of the place and the amount of fuss it had generated.

The centre had been a disused warehouse, and the black youths on the estate had begun squatting in it a few years ago, giving rise to a running dispute between the squatters on the one hand, and the police backed up by the local council on the other. The locals accused the police of harassment and brutality, while the police in their turn fulminated about drug peddling and assault. It had only come to an end when the locals finally created a management committee with Aston in the chair, and the council pumped a huge sum into reconverting the building.

With all this in mind I'd been expecting something a little more lively.

There was actually a small crowd of young men in one corner playing dominoes, and over to the right I glimpsed a lighted doorway through which a couple of boys were playing table tennis.

Walter headed for a set of stairs near the front of the room and I followed him through a doorway at the top of them into a small office.

It must have been soundproofed because the music was suddenly muted, reduced to a pulsating thud that I could feel through the soles of my feet.

The black man sitting behind the desk in the corner of the room was a bit older than the youths I'd seen downstairs. He wore a black corduroy cap with a peak, and he didn't get up to greet us, merely pushed his cap back on his head and stared up at Walter. His air wasn't hostile, but it wasn't friendly either. Just a shade outside the borderlines of welcome.

Walter greeted him and introduced me. His name was Dalton Taylor, and he acknowledged mine with a grunt and a nod of the head.

'This is the guy I told you about,' Walter said.

Dalton paid no attention to that. Instead he picked up a sheet of paper that was lying in front of him and waved it.

'It's started,' he said. 'Look at this. Fuckeries. They write me this morning asking about accounts. They want to cut us.'

Walter took the letter from him, read it quickly, then handed it back.

'Don't worry,' he said. 'I'll talk to them. See what's happening.'

'Next thing,' Dalton said, 'they'll have the police dog running through here sniffing drugs, trying to close us down.'

'We'll fight it,' Walter said. His features had taken on a sullen cast, like Dalton's and, suddenly, I realised that he was speaking with a Jamaican accent.

Dalton continued as if Walter hadn't spoken.

'I tell you one thing. The youth won't stand for it. Some of them ready to explode. They can't take no more.'

I could sense that this was a ritual which might go on and on. Part of it was clearly intended to impress me, but I'd spent too much of my life listening to people like Dalton uttering the same blend of complaint and threat.

'Excuse me, Dalton,' I said quickly. 'I don't want to take up too much of your time. I'm writing this article, like Walter told you, and I'm just trying to work out Aston's last hours, you know. Where he was and who he saw. I wondered if he'd been in touch with you or anyone had said anything to you about seeing him.'

He stared at me for what seemed a long time. Then his face switched in an instant from what looked like a mask of deep suspicion to merriment. He began to laugh, a high, cackling, crazy sound. The transformation was unnerving, but I smiled to keep him company. When I looked at Walter, he was smiling too. I wondered if he was as amused as I was, which was not at all.

'Fucking Aston,' Dalton said. He chuckled a little as if remembering a joke. 'Aston didn't use to come round here.'

'He used to hold a surgery here practically every week,' Walter said. He sound resigned rather than indignant. 'You know that.'

'Politics,' Dalton said. He got up and flexed his legs as if he was uncomfortable being seated while talking.

'He used to come here to hold on to the political base. But his real friends were somewhere else.'

He stabbed down with his finger in an emphatic gesture. He was about my height and he had a hard bulky body which made him look stocky, shorter than he was, but he moved with a fluid gracefulness that was almost hypnotic.

He felt me watching and he gazed back at me, his eyes boring into mine as if he were trying to tell me something.

'Labour Club,' he said. 'He was up there playing that left wing right wing shit. Trade union militancy. Gay politics.'

He burst out laughing again as if the whole idea was inherently ludicrous.

This time Walter didn't smile.

'You have to deal with the white left,' he said. 'Or you get nowhere.'

Dalton kept on looking at me.

'Games. Babylon full of games. Aston start getting too far into the black scene. Power. Using the estate to do his own thing. The thieves fall out, so they kill him and dump him on our doorstep. Blame a black youth. Let the Keystone cops take the pressure off them and put it back on us. Next thing they find another stooge and everything go on same as before. Games, man, games.'

He sniggered, waggled his hips and pointed to Walter.

'He's the next one. Going to Parliament, eh Walter?'

'Come on, you blood,' Walter said.

He shook his head in a resigned fashion, but there was something almost abject about it.

By contrast Dalton's pose had become increasingly aggressive; and I was also beginning to find him more and more impressive. Even if his brand of paranoiac theorising was off the wall, in this little compass he was king. He'd fought for it, possessed it and was prepared to defend it against all comers.

In spite of his alliances and contacts in the corridors of power, Walter had no such certainty or commitment.

'So you don't think Tony did it?' I asked Dalton.

He laughed again. I had started out by finding his laugh irritating. Now it was oddly reassuring.

'Sit down.' He pointed and I sat in front of the desk. He sat opposite me and leaned over confidentially. The coldness with which he first greeted me had disappeared.

'That youth couldn't do shit,' he said. 'He came here once or twice but he wasn't on the scene, you know. I know his sister Margaret, a good sister, but the brother wasn't like, hard. He spent his time up under Aston wife. Check it out.'

'What about drugs? I heard Aston was talking against drugs on the estate.'

He shrugged. Some of the suspicion came back to his expression but he responded without heat.

'There's no big dealing around here. It's just grass, sensemillia, coke, small things. Aston talked. Like let us keep drugs off the estate. Blah, blah. You think even if there was big dealing them guys would kill him for that? No. It was only talk. Politics and preaching.'

It sounded convincing enough.

'So who do you think killed him?'

His eyes flicked past me to Walter, and he smiled ironically.

'Politics,' he said. 'Let me tell you how these guys do things. Aston standing for candidate. The Asians put a man up against him. They want their own man. He's talking anti racist and gay cause he's a big batty man. All the gays and them turning to him. So Aston get this woman, Spid. She's a lesbian councillor, plenty favours go on between them. She stand to split the gay vote, and Aston coming up in front between them. Then just a few weeks ago I hear big ructions. Aston fall out with the lesbian. Big fight. I don't know the details but there was something happening. Games, man. Games.'

I looked at Walter.

'What was it?'

He shrugged the question away.

'There were a few problems. But no big fight. I didn't hear anything like that.'

Dalton leered at him. He looked back at me.

'You see how I mean?'

There didn't seem to be any point pressing Walter. Maybe I'd get more out of him on his own.

'Thanks a lot,' I told Dalton. 'I'll try and sort out all that.'

Walter said goodbye in a manner that was friendly and casual enough, but I could tell that he was angry. We went down the stairs and out of the swing doors in silence.

The music seemed quieter, or maybe my ears were simply becoming accustomed to the incessant pounding, but in any case it was a relief to be out of the building and moving away from it.

There was still an hour or so to go before closing time and I was just about to ask Walter to go for a drink so I could pump him a bit, when I heard a deep, growling voice behind us.

'Hey, Informer.'

I turned around. A little group of four youths had emerged from the building after us. At first glance I had the bizarre impression that they were all identical, then I realised that it was the effect of their close cropped haircuts with the two zigzag partings. In the same moment I recognised the two youths I'd seen that afternoon in the police station.

The one who'd spoken was a little taller than the others, and he stopped within a few feet of me, the others clustering round him in a solid block. He raised his hand and I saw that he was carrying a narrow machete.

He said it again.

'Informer.'

For the moment I had no idea what was going on, but Walter was quicker. He moved to stand a little ahead of me, his body partly blocking mine, and he threw out his hands in a puzzled gesture.

'What's going on?' he said. 'This guy's a reporter.'

'Police informer,' one of the youths who had seen me earlier said. 'He was in the station today.'

'See this,' the tall youth said. He raised the machete a little more and moved it slowly towards my face. I forced myself not to move.

'I was questioning the police,' I said loudly and firmly. 'That's my job, man. Asking about the murder.'

I watched the machete.

'Murder? What murder?'

I had the sense that he wasn't interested in the reply. His eyes were shot with red and firmly fixed on me. I stared back at him, keeping his hands as best I could in the periphery of my sight.

'Aston,' Walter said. 'I asked him to come and write about Aston. That's why he was questioning the police.'

The door banged and Dalton appeared. He strolled up to the man with the machete.

'What go on?' he asked with a coolness I could only admire.

He didn't wait for an answer, instead he put his arm round the youth's shoulders. He laughed with the now familiar high cackle.

'The guy came to see me. Rap. Take it easy.'

He turned and began leading the boy away, back towards the building. The others followed, but even with Dalton's arm round him, my adversary kept his head turned so that his eyes stayed on me, as if he was branding my features on his brain and making me a horrible promise about what he would do if he saw me again.

'Come on,' Walter said beside me, 'for Christ's sake.'

He walked hurriedly away, and I fell into step beside him.

'What was all that about?' I asked him.

'That was the Retaliators.'

'Retaliators?'

'That's what they call themselves.'

Now he mentioned it I remembered seeing the name spray-painted on the estate walls as I drove in earlier.

'Most of the black kids around here will do what they're told by the Retaliators,' Walter said. 'It's not good to get on the wrong side of them.'

'What about Aston?'

We'd reached the spot where the cars were parked.

'He had a working relationship with them.'

'Through Dalton?'

'Yes.'

He paused and thought for a moment.

'Dalton always denies it, but he's the one who tells them more or less what to do.'

'So he could be lying. About the drugs.'

Walter made an irritable gesture.

'I don't know,' he said. He made an irritated gesture. 'Look, I've got to go. Telephone me.'

He hurried away from me without waiting to hear my reply, and I watched him climb into his car and speed away. I looked around. I could still hear the music from the youth centre and for some reason I remembered the coloured lights aimlessly circling the darkened hall. I'd had a vague idea of looking round the estate but the memory made me think that was something I would want to do during the day or perhaps not at all.

I unlocked the car and got in. As I strapped myself in I took a last look at the spot where Aston had been found. In a few weeks I'd probably go past it without recognition. I hoped I wouldn't but that was how things went.

'Cheerio, mate,' I muttered.

Chapter 8

'I'm glad you're back,' I told Sophie.

I was making coffee in the little kitchen of my flat. She hung round my neck from behind, leaning on me smoochily and moving when I moved. It made the operation difficult, but after she'd been away so long the feel of her body against my back was reassuring.

'I'm sorry about your friend,' she whispered.

She kissed the back of my neck and I turned to rub my cheek against hers. The gesture was automatic, but there was something about her that worried me a little. Usually she was more talkative and less demonstrative. The difference made me wary.

Back in the sitting room she sprawled on the sofa and smiled at me affectionately. She was wearing a short black skirt, which made her legs look naked and endless. On top of that was a loose silk blouse, with a row of shiny buttons down the front.

'Where'd you get the skirt?' I asked her.

'Madrid.' She gave it a comically exaggerated Spanish pronunciation.

'You look different. Spanish, Italian? Something European. Maybe it's your hair.'

She gave me a puzzled look, but I was sure that it was an act. When I first met her she'd had curly black hair. Now it was brown with light gold streaks, and the way she looked had changed, from a recognisable Latin American with a hefty dash of African blood, to someone indeterminately Mediterranean.

'Enjoy yourself?'

She cocked her head reflectively.

'Yes.' She looked away from me. 'I had the feeling that I didn't want to come back.'

I had no reply. It didn't surprise me but I hadn't expected her to say it. She had been born in Buenos Aires, the daughter of a Scotsman and a mulatto tango dancer. I'd met her not long after she'd arrived in Britain, and even though she was British she'd talked about herself as an exile, someone cast away in a cold and friendless place. She still spoke English with a slight accent, and I suspected that she did it on purpose, as if she was trying to assert something about herself.

Everything she said now about Europe would be designed to remind me that she wasn't stuck here on what she called the narrow little island. Like me.

'What about you? What's been happening?'

I told her most of what I'd been doing the last couple of days, and she listened with an animated seriousness which told me that she thought of all this as familiar territory.

Sometimes, when she got together with friends from Argentina or other parts of Latin America, they could talk about what they called politics for hours, running down a seemingly endless list of people who'd died in mysterious circumstances or disappeared or been imprisoned. At those times they seemed almost to sparkle with energy, as if the recital fuelled their zest for life.

'I've got some pictures of him,' she said. 'I took them out of my files and brought them for you.'

The coincidence wasn't surprising. During the last year she'd been trying to establish herself as a freelance, taking every job she could find, snapping everyone and everything, and she now had in her flat two filing cabinets full of her subjects.

She dug into her bag and handed me a couple of prints.

'I only printed these. I took them during that conference

about the inner cities. But no one wanted them.'

The first one showed Aston sitting at the back of a hall in a row of empty seats. He was leaning back listening to a young woman who was speaking into his ear. She was blonde, with an intense, pretty, young face.

I looked at the picture closely. At first glance the scenario looked ordinary enough, then I realised that the girl had an expression of slightly goofy adoration, the sort of look I was used to seeing on groupies or sometimes on women who worked for powerful men. Her hand seemed to be resting on his shoulder for balance but her fingers were curled and digging in, crumpling the fabric of his suit.

In his turn Aston was smiling. I'd seen him at public meetings before, and he was usually as cheerful as the occasion allowed, but this was a private, luxurious grin. Looking at his face I would have been ready to bet that whatever the girl was whispering to him, it wasn't about council business.

The next picture had Aston in three-quarter profile, talking to a woman sitting alongside him. She was wearing a leather jacket and her black hair was cut short in a chunky punkish style. The girl was sitting back behind them, and she'd now retreated into an air of polite attention. In this pose she looked even younger and prettier.

Aston's arm was stretched out along the seat in front of her, and I had the sense that she was looking at it, and wanting to touch him.

'Macho,' Sophie said admiringly.

That was a tease too. She knew very well that the English didn't use the word that way.

'Who were these other people?' I asked her.

'The girl I don't know,' she said. 'The older woman she was a councillor too. A name like Fred. Maybe not that, but something strange.'

'Spid?'

'That's it. Spid. What sort of name is that?'

'When was this?'

'About six months ago.'

I studied the pictures again. Somehow I had the feeling that if only I could work out what they were saying I would know the answer to the mystery of Aston's death.

'Perhaps,' Sophie said, 'when you do your article they might be interested in the pictures. I have some negatives with one or two good shots of him.'

That was the nearest I came that evening to being angry with her. She'd been a photographer when we met, but in the last year or so her responses had begun to remind me of camera freaks I'd known, the sort who experienced life through the lens of a camera, so that the most important aspect of any event was the picture they'd taken.

On the other hand being a struggling freelance meant that you couldn't be choosy about what you put up for sale.

'I don't know,' I told her. 'What did you think about this girl?' I waved the photos. 'They look sort of intimate.'

'Yes,' she said with a sudden eagerness. She sat up and looked at the print. 'I wanted to get that quality. I even thought of a soft focus in the background.'

She was primarily, and perhaps only, interested in the pictures. I laughed, and she looked round at me smiling.

'Give us a kiss,' I said.

Sophie's bleeper sounded at about five in the morning. She got up, went into the next room and I heard her voice on the telephone. Then she came back and told me she had to go off to Heathrow. I grunted, and in a moment she was gone.

I went back to sleep and dreamt that I was being chased by a gang of witches. In the last horror movie I'd seen the hero had kept them off by waving a cross and shouting a liturgy, but just as I was about to employ the same tactics I realised that I didn't possess a cross and that I couldn't remember a prayer.

When I woke up again it was already ten and the rush hour traffic was still in full swing, its sounds blurred and hissing in the wet.

I rang Walter, and the woman who answered told me he was in a meeting. She sounded both pleased and stern about it, as if that would teach me not to go about ringing up important persons. I asked her when he'd be free and she said he'd be tied up until after lunch. I thanked her, hung up the phone and sat down for a think.

Nothing was obvious except the fact that I ought to start writing the article about Aston, and I sat down in front of the typewriter with a determination that made me feel strong and virtuous.

Three cups of coffee and an hour later all I had was a couple of lines which I threw at the wastepaper basket with a feeling of relief. I didn't yet know where I wanted the article to go and it had responded by digging its heels in and refusing to move.

I rang Walter and got the same woman with the same message.

That was enough for me. Sometime during the last hour my determination had hardened. Walter would see me today, even if I had to stand outside his office and bellow his name.

Less than an hour later I was walking into the lobby of the civic centre. I'd been there before, for a press conference, but even so the experience gave me a strange dislocated feeling. When I lived nearby, as a boy, the town hall was a Victorian building, a larger version of the public library, clad in red brick and civic dignity. Now it was a beehive of smoky glass and blond wood.

I kept feeling that somehow I'd got into the wrong building.

Walter's office was at the end of a corridor on the second floor overlooking a car park. It was room 29 but a notice on the door said that you had to go to room 28. I went back along the corridor, knocked and went in.

It was a big room. Several desks were scattered around but I could only see four people. The one nearest the door, a middle-aged Indian woman, had a name plate in front of her which said that she was F. Ghosh, secretary of the press unit. I said hello and waited till she glanced up at me.

'Can I help you?' she asked. Her expression said that such a thing was unlikely.

I told her that I wanted to see Walter. She asked me if I had an appointment. I said I didn't.

'He's busy all day,' she said.

She went back to her typing as if she'd solved the problem and the next time she looked up I'd be gone. I stayed where I was, smiling nicely at her.

In about a minute she eyed me again, her expression a nice blend of anger and resignation.

'There's no point in waiting, he's busy.'

'Well. I'll wait anyway.'

She smiled grimly.

'I'm sorry but you can't stand there. This isn't a waiting room.'

We stared at each other. Her voice had turned shrill and scratchy and for a moment I wondered whether she had instructions from Walter to keep me out, but I was sure that she was being awkward on general principles. People who wandered in and tried to see the boss without an appointment had to be kept in their place.

I don't know what would have happened but at that point the door next to the secretary opened and Walter poked his head out.

'Hi Sammy,' he said, as if he'd expected me to be standing there.

I nodded casually, falling into the spirit of the thing.

'I won't be a minute,' he said.

There was a bustling, slightly self-important air about him which had a distinct effect on the atmosphere of the office. F. Ghosh had suddenly lost her officious manner and acquired an accommodating, almost sycophantic smile which Walter ignored. Instead he gave her a few instructions in a curt soft voice and turned away abruptly.

'Come on, Sammy,' he said and went through the door of his room without looking back.

In spite of myself I was more or less impressed. It hadn't

occurred to me that Walter was the sort of person who could cow his staff so easily, and as I followed him into his office I found myself reassessing the man.

On the way I gave the secretary my nicest smile but the look she gave me in return was only just short of a glare.

'I've only got a few minutes,' Walter said immediately. 'What's up?'

I got out the photo Sophie had given me and showed it to him. He looked at it for a long time without saying anything and eventually I lost patience.

'Who are they?'

'I don't think they're anything to do with it,' he said.

'I don't suppose they are,' I told him, 'but I want to know.'

He shot me an impatient look from beneath his eyebrows, but when he spoke it was in a reasonable tone.

'This is Kim Parker,' he pointed to the younger one, 'and the other one is Spid Tarrant. She's a councillor.'

'She the gay councillor Dalton was on about?'

'Yes.'

The word came out reluctantly. Our eyes met and he looked away.

'What about the other one? Kim. Who is she?'

'She was doing some research for him.'

'She's very young. A whiz kid?'

Walter looked uncomfortable.

'Not exactly. She was okay. She dropped out of university. She had some trouble. I don't know. She was supposed to be going back in a year's time. Aston gave her a job in the meantime.'

'How come he didn't give a black kid the chance? In the circumstances.'

Walter was silent for a moment.

'She's one of the Parkers,' he said. As if that explained it all.

'The Parkers?'

He looked impatient again.

'Keith Parker. He's a building contractor. We do a lot of business with him. He's also a big man in the local party.'

'Nepotism.'

'Don't use words like that. She was around and she could do the job.'

'Was Aston doing her?'

Walter finally lost patience.

'Look, I don't know anything about that. You're supposed to be writing a serious story and you're wasting time. I've got plenty to do, man.'

'All right,' I said, remembering the other things I had to ask him about. 'Just a couple of more questions. These other people who were standing for the nomination.'

'Spid Tarrant, Vijay Prashad and Kevin Sparks. They're all councillors.'

'Right. I want to get some quotes from them about Aston. Where do I find them?'

He looked happier.

'They're all in, I think. There's a sub-committee. Is that it?'

'Can you ask them to see me?'

He sat down behind his desk and picked up the phone.

I turned away and while he talked softly into the phone I began looking at the photos on the wall. They were all more or less the sort of pictures you'd expect a political aspirant to have. Walter with the Mayor, Walter with Aston, Walter in a group round Neil Kinnock.

'You're looking good,' I told him when he put the phone down.

He acknowledged the compliment with a grunt which covered a smile of pure pleasure.

'You can go up and see Vijay and Kevin now. Spid's a bit busy.'

'When can I see her?'

He frowned.

'I don't know. She said you ought to ring her for an appointment sometime next week.'

'Next week? That's too late, man.'

'That's what I told her,' he said. 'But she wouldn't budge.'

'She's trying to duck me. Right? She doesn't want to talk. Do you think she's worried about what I might find out?'

'Don't jump to conclusions,' Walter said hurriedly. 'It doesn't mean that necessarily. You just never know with her.'

I didn't push it. I suspected that even though Walter probably trusted me as much as he was going to trust anyone connected with the Press, he was still as nervous as a cat about the whole affair. It wouldn't take much to put him right off helping me.

'Okay,' I said. 'I'll go and see those other guys now.'

He told me where to find them and I thanked him and went to the door. Then I remembered something else.

'By the way. What sort of research was Kim doing for Aston?'

He looked at me suspiciously, but I was wearing an expression of innocent enquiry.

'Nothing special. Checking facts. Writing letters asking for information. Ringing people.'

I had more questions about that, but I thought they would wait, so I waved at him and went out.

Chapter 9

Vijay was waiting for me. His office was on the next floor and when I came up the stairs he was standing in the corridor outside an open door.

He was a stocky little bouncing ball of a man, but he had the same anxious look I remembered. In the days when black politics had been a matter of protest marches and meetings, Vijay had always been around, voluble and bustling, wearing that harassed expression, but someone must have told him because he'd grown a short beard which made his face look a little calmer.

'Sammy,' he said. 'You're still alive. People keep asking me what happened to you.'

'As you see,' I said. 'Trying to earn a living.'

My stock answer. Over the last ten years I'd dropped out of the circle of people who organised the meetings, raised the money, sat on the committees and made speeches. It wasn't that I'd stopped believing in the same things. It was something to do with getting older and watching the same events recurring, calling up the same well-rehearsed indignation over and over again, hanging out with the same people, saying the same things in the same words. It had been a busy little rut, but the more I did the deeper it had seemed to get.

Vijay led the way into an office, which was double the size of Walter's, already talking.

'I can't tell you anything about what happened to Aston,' he said. 'As a matter of fact I don't know much about what he was doing lately. I just saw him at meetings.'

'What did you disagree about?'

He'd just sat down behind his desk, but he looked up sharply at that.

'Whoa,' he said. 'Don't start that, Sammy. We didn't disagree. We just have different interests. That's why I was up for the nomination.'

'Your chances must have improved.'

He shrugged. His little red eyes burned into mine. Then he looked away.

'I couldn't tell you. I haven't thought about it yet.' He slapped the desk with his hand. 'Anyway, I can't tell you about all that. I don't know what Aston was doing and I don't care. I thought you were writing an article about how the politics in the borough had changed and Aston's part in it.'

'That's right.'

'Right. I'll tell you about what's been happening the last few years.'

I pretended to be taking notes while Vijay talked, but what he had to say was a familiar history.

They had built a faction, partly by accident, partly by design. Aston was a focus, drawing activists into the party, registering voters, dominating meetings. After the local elections they were part of a ruling majority. The papers called them the loony Left, but that was only sour grapes. They were in possession.

The recital made me uneasy. I had been involved in some of it, but when I thought of the endless meetings, and the sheer amount of time they must have spent doing what they did, it gave me the creeps. Worse. There was a bit of guilt in my reaction. Whatever I thought of Vijay, at least he and the others had lived the logic of their beliefs.

'How come you were standing against Aston?'

Vijay leaned forward, staring at me.

'Things have changed you know. We don't have to pretend

differences don't exist. Aston and me, we're different people, we represent different things.'

You mean different races, I thought.

'So I heard,' I said.

I'd been hoping to sting him into a reaction, but although his expression grew a little more agitated, he wasn't going to be provoked.

'Everybody knows that,' he said. He looked at his watch. 'I've got to go, Sammy.'

I got up. I'd taken up nearly an hour of his time, but in the old days Vijay had been the sort of person who grabbed you and talked until you prised yourself away. It was obvious that a lot had changed.

I said my goodbyes quickly and set out down the corridor for Kevin Sparks' room, and I'd already walked several yards when I realised that I'd seen Spid Tarrant's name on a door across the corridor. I went back and knocked. Nothing happened, so I knocked again, and when I heard a woman's voice shouting something indistinct, I turned the knob and walked in.

She was sitting near the window looking out. Something sad and reflective in her pose suggested that she'd been sitting there for a long time, deep in thought; and when she looked at me her eyes were blurred and vague. I had the sudden and uncanny feeling that I knew her well.

'Hello, Ms Tarrant,' I said.

I'd been working on a better opening line, but my brain seemed to have seized up.

Her gaze sharpened and struck at me.

'Who are you? What do you want?'

I started to tell her who I was, but she interrupted as soon as she heard my name.

'I told Walter I couldn't see you,' she said. 'What's going on? What's your game?'

'I just saw your name on the door and I thought I'd look in. See if you were free.'

'Well I'm not. You're wasting your time anyway. I don't

know what happened to Aston and if I did I'd tell the police, not the gutter press.'

I opened my mouth to tell her that I wasn't the gutter press, but before I could get the words out she was bellowing at me.

'Get out. Or I'll call security. Get out.'

I couldn't think of anything to say that would help so I got out. As I closed the door I remembered why her face was familiar. A few months before this one of the tabloids had done an exposé about lesbians in high places, and Spid's features, staring out from between the newsprint in blank surprise, had been famous for a couple of days. I hadn't done my homework or I'd have known how she would react. She was going through the selection process and any bad press coverage would probably mean disaster.

The problem was that sooner or later I'd have to speak to her, and now it was probably going to be impossible.

Suddenly the entire enterprise seemed useless and without pausing I headed for the nearest staircase down to the lobby. In the same moment I heard someone call out my name.

'Mr. Dean?'

I looked round. In my confusion I had walked past Kevin Sparks' room, and now he was standing by the open door looking at me with a mixture of puzzlement and irritation.

'Come in. Come in,' he said. 'I was waiting for you.'

I walked into the room behind him, struggling to concentrate.

'I put some documents together for you when Walter rang me,' he said.

Concealing my surprise, I leafed through the papers he pushed across the desk. They turned out to be xeroxed copies of a couple of speeches and a short CV.

'That's just a bit of background,' he said.

'Interesting,' I said seriously, turning the pages and pretending to read.

In reality I was looking at him and trying to adjust. Something about him made me uneasy and, still thinking about my encounter with Spid, I wondered whether I'd also seen his picture in the papers. Then as he opened his mouth to speak, I got it.

One of my first teachers in secondary school had looked exactly like this. Ginger hair, pale skin, deep-set greenish eyes. Even the clothes, a tweedy old jacket, woollen tie and corduroy trousers, looked the same. He too had been a Labour party activist, given to long explanations of phrases like 'the crisis of capitalism' during English lessons. During my fourth year he had targeted me, for some reason, and given me the *The Ragged Trousered Philanthropists* to read, but I'd been too embarrassed to tell him that I'd read it a year earlier. 'Sir's bumboy,' Borelli had sneered, daring me to fight.

Suddenly I realised that he had asked me something about the article I was writing and was waiting for an answer. Gathering my thoughts I told him the story I'd rehearsed with Walter. He nodded seriously but I had the impression he was merely confirming what he already knew, and I sensed also that he could hardly wait for me to stop so that he could begin speaking. Spid had been a burnt child, but this man was a real politician who knew the value of a few column inches.

'Aston was a great comrade,' he said, 'but there were always problems about the race issue.'

I put an astonished look on my face.

'Oh yeah,' he said. 'I'll be frank. I think we've suffered a great loss and I admired him more than anyone but the way some people around here are talking you'd think he was the only one who was fighting racism in the borough. We all played our part.'

I waited for him to tell me what an outstanding role he'd played, but mercifully he didn't go into details.

'Is that why you were standing against him for the candidacy?'

He frowned angrily.

'Of course not. It's a democratic right. You can't make a story out of that.'

'I wasn't trying to,' I said. 'I'm just trying to get a picture of where he was politically.'

He leaned forward.

'Well, that's interesting. You know about the youth centre?'

I nodded non-committally.

'If Aston had any real enemies that's where they were. It's a difficult situation down there. He was looking into it.'

'What do you mean?'

He gazed at me for a moment, sizing me up. By now I had a grip on some of his mannerisms. This direct stare of his seemed to indicate uncertainty. A good disguise.

'They have a lot of problems. Drugs. Vandalism, violence.'

He paused, and I thought it was a good moment to gee him up a little.

'There's nothing unusual about that.'

'No. But there was another real problem.'

He hesitated again, and suddenly I had the sense that these pauses were nothing to do with a reluctance to talk. He was psyching me up. Impressing on me how important what he had to say was.

'You can't quote me on this, but a lot of money went missing from the project.'

'Go on.'

He nodded soberly.

'There were rumours but the auditor only got on to it a few weeks ago. He went straight to the treasurer.'

'What happened?'

Underneath his concerned expression there was a quick flash of something that looked like pleasure, then it was gone.

'There could have been a number of reasons. Maybe inefficiency. Poor management. Book keeping is always difficult for these community groups. They gave it a little while. Aston said he'd see whether he could clear things up. Whatever it was.'

'Then he was killed.'

'I'm not drawing any conclusions,' he said. 'It's too soon for that.'

If that was so I wondered why he was telling me all this.

'Even so,' I said. 'Do you feel the money was anything to do with it?'

He shrugged.

'I don't know. The finance committee is sorting it out. It all depends on what they find out. That's all I can tell you.'

'Anything else? About Aston I mean.'

He looked puzzled.

'I don't know. It's a great loss. Not just to the black community, but to everyone else as well.'

He looked almost distressed when he said that. But I wondered whether he meant it. He struck me as the type who was thorough about acting the details of the image he was trying to put over. He would look sad when he was supposed to. When the time came for joy he would look joyful. It was a politician's mask behind which anything could be happening.

With that thought came the suspicion that I was wasting my time trying to find out anything that he didn't want to tell me, and in any case I had quite enough to think about. I put my hands on the arms of the chair and levered myself upright.

He must have been expecting it, because he got up at the same time and we shook hands with what, I guessed, was about the same amount of hypocrisy.

'Thank you very much for your time,' I said, smiling warmly.

Chapter 10

I came out the civic centre into a weak afternoon sun, nostalgia tearing at me like a dog's teeth.

A little knot of boys in school uniform brushed past and ran into the tube station on the corner. Without thinking about it I paused, gazing after them. Twenty years ago the façade had been clean and new. It hadn't changed a lot and a picture of myself walking past this spot kept slipping in and out of my mind, one image blurring uncontrollably into another. In the same moment I remembered that this was also the spot where a white man had leaned out of his car and spat on my sister on her way home from school.

Back in the car I switched the engine on, then switched it off again. The trouble was that I didn't know what to do next. I had enough to write the article but I'd known all that from the beginning. What I really wanted, I knew now, was to find out who had killed Aston and why. Sometime during the last couple of days I'd put Eva's son, Tony, out of my mind as a suspect, but that didn't get me a lot further. Spid's reaction had raised all kinds of possibilities, but I couldn't think how to find out more.

Feeling a little desperate I got out of the car and walked back to the civic centre. I rang Walter from the reception desk.

He picked up the phone immediately and I told him about

my encounter with Spid. He didn't seem surprised.

'I'll talk to her,' he said.

'One other thing I forgot to ask you. Kim Parker's number.'

'Why? She's nothing to do with this.'

'Come on, Walter. You know the biz. I need to sling in a few quotes. She worked with him.'

There was a pause while he thought about it.

'Hang on a minute,' he said eventually.

I hung on. Across the lobby there was a huge poster detailing the good work the council was doing on behalf of the voters. Along the margins were the photos of various committee chairs, all wearing suitably grim and determined expressions. Aston's picture was among them and I guessed that Walter hadn't yet had enough time to think about changing it. I was still reading the poster when he came back on.

'There's two numbers here.'

I guessed he was reading some kind of file card.

'Let's have them both.'

He gave them to me.

'One of them is probably her parents.'

'Let's have the addresses.'

He sounded reluctant but he gave them to me.

'Go careful, Sammy,' he said at the end.

'I'm always careful.'

'I know, but this is different. You're up to something, but watch how you mess with these people.'

'Don't worry,' I said reassuringly. 'I'll watch it.'

There was a phone booth nearly opposite the entrance to the civic centre. It was littered with the usual graffiti. A dead pigeon lay in one corner flanked by two whisky bottles. I kept the door propped open with one foot and rang the first number Walter had given me.

A young woman's voice told me that she wasn't available but that I could leave a message. That was enough. There wasn't anything I wanted to say but at least the machine had confirmed the address. A quarter of an hour later I was in front of Kim's flat.

This wasn't one of the posh areas in the borough, but it was one of those streets where the tall Edwardian terraces provided the potential for a feverish process of renovation and redevelopment. Some of the houses were clad in new brick and the front gardens were once again sprouting roses and fuchsias.

Godfrey, my best friend at school, used to live two doors down from where my car was parked. Looking at the house I remembered the running battles his parents used to have with the neighbours, an elderly white couple who lived alone, and who complained continually. The smells, the noise, the mess. In those days my friend's house was always full of the relations who kept turning up from Jamaica, and the garden was full of the detritus of their coming and going, packing cases, an abandoned pram and a smashed-up sink unit.

Now it was all gone. Instead, an estate agent's placard shoved its way up out of the hedge. There must be some magic about London, I thought as I crossed the street, which, in a few years, could turn immigrant slums into prime real estate.

There were three bells and the one at the bottom said Kim Parker. I rang and nothing happened. I rang again, then moved over to try peering through the chink in the curtains.

Behind me there was a scuffling sound.

'What do you want?' a woman's voice said.

I turned round, moving slowly so as not to alarm her, and saw a short, thin, middle-aged white woman, who was looking at me with a mixture of annoyance and apprehension. She was holding the leashes of two cream-coloured Labradors but she stood with her weight balanced on one leg, as if poised to run.

'I'm looking for Kim Parker,' I said immediately. 'I'm a colleague of hers. From the town hall.'

Her expression lightened a little, but she was still suspicious.

'She's not been in, you see,' I added, 'and we thought she was sick.'

'I don't know about that, but I thought she'd gone round to her parents'. She left a couple of days ago. With suitcases.'

'Ah well,' I said, trying to look like someone from the town hall. 'We didn't know, you see.'

'I thought there might be something wrong after that man got killed. But I didn't get a chance to talk to her before she went. She left me a note. To feed the cat, but I mean it's not easy with the dogs and that.'

I could see why Kim might have avoided talking to her. Now she was sure that I wasn't a mugger or a rapist, she was obeying her prime directive. To boldly gossip, to speculate wildly about her neighbours, to talk endlessly without regard to interruption. But there had been a tiny hesitation when she mentioned that man being killed.

'The man who was killed. You mean Councillor Edwards.'

'That's him. He came here sometimes. Of course I didn't know he was a councillor to begin with when I saw him first. I knew she worked for the town hall, but I don't know anything about politics. Then I recognised him from the papers. She said he was her boss. But he used to come here all hours. That's why I thought maybe there was some trouble when I read he'd got killed. I was going to go down and ask her about it, but she'd left.'

I made a show of looking at my watch.

'I must go I'm afraid.'

As I began to cross the road she called out after me.

'If you contact her tell her about the cat. It's a bit difficult.'

I waved at her and hurried away, but she stood there watching, probably thinking of a hundred things she hadn't told me, while I started the car and pulled into the traffic.

Sitting in the rush hour queue I thought over what I had learnt. The fact that Aston visited the flat was interesting but not necessarily revealing, and it might have been a coincidence that Kim had hurried off so soon after his death, but instinct told me that it wasn't.

The Parkers' house had to be my next stop.

It was in the same area as Aston's, only a few streets away, and it was bigger, with a driveway leading to a two-car garage beside it. The front garden was laid out with flower beds arranged in a geometric order round a big flowering cherry. The picture was completed by a woman in a big hat kneeling on the edge of the crazy paving digging with a trowel. She was doing it with a practised and relaxed energy which looked professional.

She was tall, and long wavy blonde hair emerged from beneath the broad-brimmed hat she was wearing and fell down to cover her shoulders. Kim.

I got out of the car and crossed the road quickly. She ignored the car door slamming, but looked up when she heard me coming, and I saw that she was older than I'd thought, about forty perhaps. The dark glasses she was wearing made it difficult to check the resemblance, but I guessed that this had to be Kim's mother.

'Mrs Parker?'

'Yes.'

She looked and sounded nervous, but that meant nothing. In a street like this, the advent of a strange black man would make a woman like this nervous. As if to confirm my thought she glanced rapidly up and down the row of houses. Probably checking to see whether the neighbours had noticed my arrival.

'Is Kim at home?'

She frowned.

'No. She isn't.'

She stopped abruptly, and I had the feeling she had been about to tell me where her daughter was before she remembered it was a secret.

'Who are you?'

I told her who I was. Later on I thought it would have been easier and more sensible to tell her a lie, but I'd liked her on sight and I didn't feel like lying to her.

'She can't tell you anything,' she said. 'She worked for him, but she doesn't know anything about his private affairs.'

I knew now that wasn't true; I wondered whether she knew it too, but her expression, behind the dark glasses, was unreadable.

'Can you tell me where she is? I'd like to speak to her.'

'I don't know,' she said. 'She's on holiday with a friend.'

'Do you know who the friend is?'

'I'm sorry. I have to go now. None of this is anything to do with us. I'm sorry I can't help you.'

She said all this with a kind of abrupt decision, then she turned and, almost running, went back into the house.

I thought of following her but I wasn't sure what the point would be, so I got back into the car and drove away past the pretty houses and beautiful gardens. Down the road I noticed a couple of pink blossoms resting on my sleeve and I brushed them off with a feeling of something like regret.

Chapter 11

Round about eleven I was sitting in front of the telly hoping that Sophie would ring. I knew she wouldn't but something about the day had made me feel lonely and deprived. I wanted to see her even if it turned out badly.

Sometime during the evening I'd rung my son, but he was watching a video of an Arnold Schwarzenegger movie, the most wicked actor in the world, he said, and he was in a hurry to put down the phone. I looked at the news for a while but I couldn't concentrate.

The people I'd seen during the day kept walking through my head trailing questions. Why? Where was Kim and why was it a big secret? Why was her beautiful mum so nervous and frightened? Why was Spid so hostile and why had she had a row with Aston as Dalton had told me? Was Suzie hiding anything?

After a few minutes of this I sat in front of the typewriter and thought about what I was going to write. As usual the process spurred me into action, and in the moment I touched the keys I had decided to go and take a look at Kim's flat. It was such a stupid idea that I got up and ran out of the flat before I could talk myself out of it.

The glass cutter made a tiny high-pitched squeak as I drew

round the plunger where I'd stuck it to the window, and I paused in case the dogs heard it, but nothing moved. Then I jerked my wrist and the glass came free.

I placed it carefully on the ground and put my son's multi-bladed penknife back in my pocket, moving as slowly and silently as I could. I had come in over the high gate beside the house then walked through the little alleyway behind it to get into the back garden, and so far there'd been no problems, but I didn't want to take any chances.

I waited a little while before reaching through the hole in the glass and unscrewing the window catch. A moment later I was inside.

Standing there in the dark I felt a rush of excitement so massive that it was as if my blood had been pumped out and replaced by pure adrenalin. I put my hand on the window sill to steady myself and breathed deeply. It must feel something like this to be a burglar, I thought. Then it struck me. That was exactly what I was doing.

In about a minute my eyes were accustomed to the dark, but I knew where the light switch had to be, so I made my way cautiously over to the doorway and clicked it on.

I was in a bedroom. It was big enough to accommodate a double bed and leave plenty of room for me to walk from the window to the door without bumping into the dressing table against the other wall.

I looked around wondering where to start. The problem was that I didn't know what I was after. I was there because I'd had a strong sense that Kim was somehow connected to Aston's death, and her disappearance made it feel like a certainty, but now I was in her bedroom it was hard to concentrate.

The trouble was that it was a neat spare room with nothing much in it except clothes and furniture. In a couple of glances I'd seen it all. On the table beside the bed there was a photo of Aston in his office smiling into the camera. It looked like a publicity photo. Next to it was the surprise.

A snap of Kim sitting on a sofa with an older woman who had her arms round her. They were grinning affectionately at each other, and it might have been one of those mother and daughter photos, only it wasn't.

I shook my head and studied it closely to make sure that the other woman was Spid. A revelation. Or maybe it wasn't. On the other hand, if it meant that Kim had been involved with both Aston and Spid, all kinds of possibilities opened up.

Above me there was a scuffling noise that I realised must be the dogs. They must have known I was there by now and one of them began to bark. An urgent, angry sound.

I slipped the photo into my pocket and went through the door into the passage and eased into the front room. Above me I could hear the dogs snarling and scuffling and I switched the light on before I thought about whether anyone might see it.

This room was bigger. A television. A sofa. One armchair. In the corner near the window was a big desk, and I went straight to it.

It had the same tidied-up neatness as the bedroom. An electric typewriter in the middle. A couple of files in a neat rectangle. Next to them a little pile of books, and a small square tray with pens in it. No mess. No clutter. This girl was so neat. At the back of my mind the thought flickered that she couldn't be the sort of person who would get into the sexual entanglements I imagined. I pushed it away and opened the first drawer.

A letter lying on top of a small stack of stationery, as if she'd opened it, read it and tossed it in there. I took it out and then opened the next two drawers. Typing paper, a row of files. Nothing interesting. I shut the drawers and picked up the letter, weighing it in my hand. It was odd. I'd broken into the flat, searched it and now I was hesitating about reading her letters.

The barking upstairs started again. Double the volume now as the other dog joined in. Then the woman's voice, shouting at them. I hadn't seen the cat, but if she was looking after it, she'd probably have a key.

The flat began to feel like a trap, the walls getting smaller. I put the letter in my pocket and turned to go, then the books on the desk caught my eye. The top one, bound in shiny brown leather, had, for some reason, struck me as a Bible or a book of poems, but when I took a closer look I could see that it was some sort of diary. I picked it up with a feeling of triumph. The first page was an address written in a firm regular hand, the strokes clear and rounded.

A door slammed somewhere and the noise of the dogs' barking grew louder. In for a penny. I shoved the diary into my pocket and went for the safety of the bedroom and the open window.

Once outside I negotiated the passage with no trouble, slipping the bolt on the gate and squeezing through to the garden. Then over the wall into the front of the next house. As I got into the street I looked back and saw that the flat above Kim's now had the lights on. I guessed that by now the dogs' owner would be downstairs looking for an intruder. I wondered how long it would take her to discover the hole in the window and what she would do.

It didn't matter now.

Chapter 12

I began flipping through the diary under the street lights in the High Street. It was such good handwriting that I could read it easily, but I was too strung up, still flying with the effect of all that adrenalin. So I contented myself with looking at the last entries for a clue to Kim's whereabouts and, as if by magic when I turned to the day's entry, there was an address. When I looked a little closer I realised that there was a time under it. A dinner party perhaps or a meeting with a friend. On the other hand, it said 'after 10', so it was most likely to be some sort of party.

That was just fine, I thought. I was right in the mood for a party, and if Kim was there I could probably talk to her unobtrusively. I reached for the A–Z and looked up the street.

It was the Bohemian end of the borough. Here the old art college marked the boundary where bed-sitter land shaded into residential housing. Hippies used to hang out here, and in the next street I'd got drunk on pale ale and maraschino cherries at my first teenage party. The cherries couldn't have had much to do with it, but it was years before I could look at a bottle of them without feeling sick. It was here too that Val Owen, a fifteen-year-old with brilliant blue eyes and big breasts, had asked me round to keep her company while her parents were out. Next day a Ted in 4c named Arthur, who claimed to be her boyfriend, cornered me in the school toilets and, aided by five of his mates, punched both my eyes closed before I was rescued.

Val hadn't had the same effect on me as the cherries, but both experiences had begun to teach me the limitations that surrounded what I could do.

The area didn't seem to have changed much, unless you took account of its tolerance for noise, because, as soon as I opened the door of the car, I could hear the party music and the sound of a houseful of people having themselves a ball, even though I'd parked a long way up the street.

On the way I'd begun to worry about getting in, but as I approached the door a couple walked up to it, pushed it open and went in. Simple. Inside there was a long hallway choked with people. I struggled down it smiling vaguely around me, trying to concentrate on the faces. The hallway ended in a kitchen, and I began working my way back. The drink would be in the front room, I guessed, but I was a little chary of walking straight in and beginning to booze it up. Mentally I kicked myself for not bringing a bottle.

'Hello, sweetie,' a strange voice said behind me. 'Slumming it?'

I looked round, but I didn't recognise either of the two men behind me. One of them had made a mess of his lipstick and it was smeared all over his mouth, giving him a peculiar, crazy air. Both of them had dark shadows showing through their make-up, like circus clowns.

I grinned at them, winked, and took the nearest avenue of escape, up the stairs, resolving to look in the front room later. The men were wearing dresses and being up front about it, which must mean that it was a gay party, but on my way up I kept on bumping into women and if any of them were transvestites I couldn't spot it.

It wasn't until I had made my way into the front room on the first floor, where they were dancing, that I realised apart from the odd man and the two downstairs everyone I'd seen so far was female. In front of me the dancers were closely entwined, heads on shoulders, face to face. In one corner two women were kissing passionately.

Another fine mess. I'd assumed that the curious looks I was getting were to do with me being a stranger among them, but actually I must have stuck out like a flashing neon sign. If I kept on striding about gazing at the women they'd probably sling me out on my ear, and even if I found Kim, she certainly wouldn't greet me with open arms. I turned to leave.

'Following me around, are you?'

A hand on my arm. I turned round cautiously, and saw Spid Tarrant, her face flushed and contorted with anger.

'Following me around?'

'No. I'm not,' I said in what I hoped was a soothing tone. 'As a matter of fact I'm looking for Kim Parker. Is she here?'

'You're pathetic,' she said contemptuously. She'd raised her voice and the women were gathering round to look. 'Kim's a hundred miles away. Who're you working for? *News of the World*? The *Sun*?'

There was disgusted murmur round me.

'Get him out,' a shrill voice shouted.

'I'm not,' I said firmly. 'You know what I'm doing.'

'Piss off,' she said.

'I'm going,' I told her.

'Just piss off,' she said.

I pissed off. Halfway down the stairs I went past a black woman pulling a white teenager with a punk haircut behind her, and I recognised Eva's daughter, Margaret, with a slight sense of shock but not much surprise.

She'd looked startled when she saw me, and in a moment I heard her calling out after me as I ploughed through the hallway, but I took no notice. She caught up with me though. Just outside the door.

'Wait a minute. I want to talk to you.'

I stopped and she drew me to the other end of the little front garden, by the side of the house.

'Don't say anything about seeing me here to my mum.'

'I wasn't going to. Who you hang out with is your business.'

She looked around and turned back to me.

'I don't give a toss what you think,' she said. 'But my mum has problems with my way of life, and I don't want her upset, especially now.'

'You don't want her upset. Got that.'

She made a disgusted sound and I thought she was going to say something abusive, but she merely spun round and went back into the house.

I was still wondering about Eva and what she thought about Margaret when I reached the pavement, so it was a moment before I noticed the little group of women blocking my path. I moved out to walk around them, but one of them, bigger and taller than the others, stepped sideways to get in my way again.

'You dickhead,' she said.

She had a short haircut and blunt features, and when she said the word she thrust her face forward so that I got the full value of her nasty sneering grin.

'What?'

She said it again.

'Dickhead.'

There three of them and they were all wearing jeans and black leather jackets decorated with lots of zips and metal objects, and at first I thought the jingling sound came from them, but in a few seconds I realised that the big one was holding some sort of chain at waist level. From time to time she shook it suggestively.

'Come off it,' I said. 'I'm going home.'

'You bloody are,' she said.

The funny thing was that even though she was trying to talk like a street thug, she had a recognisably middle class Home Counties accent, and, actually, she sound quite refined.

'Who do you think you are?'

This one was wearing a peaked hat, and she had a pretty face with straight regular features, but with her narrowed eyes and compressed lips she looked like a young Nazi. She sounded, though, like a native North Londoner and she spoke with an exaggerated and aggressive reasonableness, a style with which Labour party branch meetings had made me familiar.

'You've no right to follow people around trying to dig up dirt for the gutter press. You should know better.'

'Sure,' I said. 'I'll go home and think about it. Okay?'

'He thinks he's funny,' the big one said.

I sensed that she was working herself up into a fury and I moved backwards to try and get between the nearest parked cars so that I could cross the road.

Without warning she swung the chain at my face, but she did it with a slow underarm movement that I could see coming a mile away. I leaned in and took her wrist in my left hand, pulled her to me and ended the move by bending her arm behind her back. I watched the others over her shoulder. The woman in the peaked hat took her right hand out of her pocket and held it up. A knife blade sprang out.

'Let her go,' she said.

I felt like laughing. If they'd known anything about it, they would all have piled in and duffed me up, instead of standing back waiting to see what happened.

'Put the knife away,' I said, 'and I'll let her go.'

'Bastard,' the one I was holding said in my ear. She tried to bite me and I twisted her arm further up her back so that she bent away from me. She shrieked, and the peaked hat shouted.

'I said let her go.'

She shuffled forward and took a tentative stab at my face. I dug my chin into the leather upholstery in front of me and kicked her in the knee. It connected a bit more solidly than I intended, and she went down squealing. The other woman bent over her and began tugging her to her feet.

A window went up above us and a woman's voice shouted.

'I'm calling the police now.'

The window banged shut, but I didn't bother to look.

'I'll let you go now,' I said.

I pushed her backwards towards her friends and she staggered a bit, then took her arm from behind her back and started rubbing it. I crossed the road, walked down to my car and got in without looking back.

The whole episode had been embarrassing, but as I drove

along I found myself chuckling. Ironically, it was probably a macho upbringing that saved me. Incapable of imagining that those awkward females could hurt me, I had reacted with a clinical precision; and that just went to show the danger of rigid mental habits, because if the women had been even moderately efficient fighters, they might have put me in hospital.

At any rate I had survived the party, but I hadn't learnt anything useful, and I hadn't located Kim. I looked at the diary lying on the seat next to me. I'd go through it at home, searching for clues.

By the time I reached the flat I was so tired that the thought of climbing the stairs loomed up in front of me like a giant obstacle course. I parked the car carefully and looked around inside it for items I intended to take upstairs.

In front of me Chummy Cholmondoley's Porsche already occupied the place just outside the door. It gleamed as if he'd just polished it, and maybe he had. Chummy was one of those kids who, still in his early twenties, was earning a fortune in the City. He had a house in Richmond where he lived with his girlfriend, and he rented the flat below mine to be near the office. He also hung out with a succession of attractive young women, but the real love of his life, I thought, was the car; he'd once confessed when we got to talking on the stairs that his main dread about leaving her parked in such an exposed spot was that, one night, a group of vandals would attack and damage her in some way.

I was just about to put the key in the lock when I heard a shoe scrape on the pavement behind me. I turned round fast. There were three of them. One of those lightning irrelevancies that come to you at crucial moments flashed through my mind. There are repetitious patterns to some days. Today everything was in threes.

This lot was led by a big blond man in a pepper-and-salt tweed jacket and blue jeans. He was flanked by two men in donkey jackets, who were even larger. They looked like the sort of men you would see standing round on building sites wearing helmets, except that they seemed fitter and harder.

'Sammy Dean? You Sammy Dean?'

I thought about denying it. I didn't know who this lot were, but the blond man had an angry look to him and I was willing to bet that they hadn't come round at this time of night to give Sammy Dean a good citizen award.

'Who wants to know?' I asked cautiously.

That was enough for him. Even under the street lamps I could see his face getting redder. He came closer and I smelt the sour stink of the alcohol on his breath. He pointed a finger in my face.

'I'm Keith Parker. I'm warning you. Leave my family alone. You upset my wife today. If you come near my house again I'm going to smash your fucking black face in, you monkey.'

I could see that he was serious, but the warning didn't worry me. What worried me was the prospect that he might decide to give me a demonstration on the spot. A few blows from these guys and I'd be half dead, then they'd kick me around to make sure I got the point. I reached back and up, keeping my hand in sight, and rang Chummy Cholmondoley's bell.

'I didn't mean to upset your wife,' I said apologetically. 'I only wanted to speak to Kim.'

'Leave my daughter alone.' His voice was lower now, but it had the force of concentrated rage. 'Don't even say her name again or I swear I'll smash you.'

He seemed near to boiling point and I put my hands up in front of me to fend him off. Just then Chummy's window went up.

'Who's there? Who's there?'

His voice had an angry, querulous note. I guessed he was looking at the donkey jackets. Knowing Chummy, I figured he'd be fantasising that the revolution had started and they'd come for his car.

''Scuse me,' I said politely to Parker. Then I pushed past him and looked up so that Chummy could see me.

'It's me, Chummy,' I shouted up at him. 'Forgot the keys. Let us in, will you?'

The window slammed shut and I turned and looked at Parker.

I had guessed that he wouldn't try anything in front of a witness, but instead of moving off he stayed where he was, his face set and hard, staring me in the eye. We stood like this until the sound of Chummy blundering against the door broke the spell. His expression changed then, and his lip curled up as if something revolting had suddenly been shoved under his nose.

'Leave my family alone,' he said, grating out each word as if he were spitting poisoned bullets. Then he turned and walked rapidly away, his two henchmen padding behind him.

'Friend of yours?' Chummy said.

He'd loitered on the stairs, waiting for me to come up. He was dying of curiosity.

'Well,' I said. 'He could be.'

Chapter 13

I woke up next morning with the feeling that something had changed. I couldn't quite put my finger on it, but it was there. Perhaps it was, I thought, the fact that the events of the previous night had shifted me from being a mere observer. Now I was part of whatever was going on. I wished I could work out, though, what that was. Keith Parker seemed a perfect candidate for any kind of violent assault. Although I'd often seen well-fed, florid men like him gibbering with anger, there'd been a gleam in his eyes which came from somewhere deep down, and which told me that his rage wasn't just provoked by the occasion. It lived permanently inside him, like an animal mad with desperation, wild and almost uncontrollable.

Then there was Spid, who seemed a touch off the wall, even for someone still smarting from being trashed by the tabloids; and there was the possibility that my interest in them was a deliberate distraction from the problem of the youth project. Perhaps I was simply shying away from the thought that a gang of black thugs had killed Aston for simple straightforward reasons, in much the same way that I found it hard to believe that young Tony was involved.

The electronic screeching of the telephone matched the vibrating jangle in my head and for a moment I let it ring because it was such a welcome interruption. When I picked it up the person on the other end sounded impatient; but then he always did.

'Is that Sammy?'

'Tommy, you old dog,' I said, 'of course it's me answering my own phone.'

'Well you never know,' he said darkly. 'That Spanish woman you got mighta moved another man into the place.'

He cackled mightily down the phone, but the way things had been between Sophie and me made it an irritating remark and I let him choke himself into silence before I replied.

'What can I do for you, Tommy?'

His mood changed immediately.

'What can you do for me? You mean if I pick up the phone and ring, you have to be asking me what I want? Let me tell you Aston never treated me like that.'

His tone was half serious, half comical exaggeration, but under it he was testing me.

'You can ring me any time. You know that, Tommy. I just wondered whether it was something special.'

He grunted, satisfied.

'I want to see you,' he said. 'About Aston.'

Even before he said it I'd been kicking myself for not thinking of Tommy before, because Tommy was Aston's personal pensioner, at least that was what we called him when we were sitting around having a giggle about the old boy's crazy ways. If anyone knew what Aston had been thinking it would be Tommy.

'Tommy,' I said. 'You're the very man I want to see.'

He grunted grudgingly.

'I heard you were snooping around, but I still had to ring you. You should have come to see me first.'

I agreed, as I usually did, because outright disagreement threw him into a rage. But that was one of his reassuring characteristics, because it reminded us of the way adults were when we were children; and Tommy served us as a sort of link between our previous lives and this one.

In those days he'd been a sailor. His mother lived in our

street, and he'd turn up at odd times during the year, distributing little packets of American chewing gum. You could always tell when Tommy was around, because all the kids would be busily chewing and talking with an American accent.

After thirty years the memory had faded, and when Aston rang to tell me that the old man had turned up at one of his meetings it took a considerable effort to work out who he was. But from that time they'd become firm friends. Tommy would visit Aston and Suzie several times a week, and lecture them on politics, the duties of a wife, the state of the world and anything else that came into his head. Suzanne was fascinated and amused by his mixture of clowning and high seriousness, while Aston could talk to him about the people and the issues he encountered every day, without the fear of his words coming back to haunt him. They'd cared about each other, and I should have remembered that Tommy would be finding Aston's death hard to bear.

The anxiety in his voice echoed my thought.

'So I'll see you today. I have to go and see the widow now, but I'll be back in the afternoon.'

He put the phone down abruptly.

The phone call gave the day an uneasy start. Another reminder that Aston used to have a generosity which drew people to him. Somehow the thought irritated me a little, and that made me wonder whether I'd been jealous of him all along. Dangerous ground, and I heard the sound of the doorbell with relief, but I let it ring a few times before it struck me that it was Saturday morning, and that meant it would be my son. Normally he'd be playing basketball at this time, but he'd hurt his leg on the court during the week, and he'd rung to say he was going to visit me instead.

He was standing there with a look of barely restrained impatience on his face. Mine. All mine. It was great to see him.

Over the last months he'd shot up, gangling into his first teenage year. I had the feeling I always had when I saw him, that somehow he'd grown when I wasn't looking. 'What a big boy,' I'd murmur admiringly, while he rolled his eyes and looked the other way.

'What took you so long, Dad?'

We spent the next couple of hours wrangling amiably about Henry the Eighth, about the merits of Arnold Schwarzenegger, about the usefulness of grammar, and about whether John Barnes was really the greatest football player England had yet produced. In between he explained to me for the umpteenth time why no other country could hope to rival American basketball players.

Round about half past twelve I'd come to a decision about something I'd been kicking around in the back of my mind.

'Let's go see Maman Nightingale,' I said.

'Who's that?'

An irritating habit he'd developed. I was sure he knew who Maman was, but absent-mindedness was a signal that he wasn't enthusiastic.

'The fat lady. You must remember.'

'Oh yeah. Why?'

'I want to see her. To ask her son, Aubrey, to help me with the story I'm working on. About Aston.'

That was true enough, even though I was leaving out the crucial bit.

'If you want, Dad.'

'You don't have to.'

He smiled.

'I said okay. If you want.'

Another signal. He thought I wanted him with me because Maman was one of those people I wanted him to know. Old friends to whom I would boast, 'This is my son.' He didn't want to, but he didn't mind.

Sometimes his patience and tolerance with me were infuriating. I wanted him to know and to understand the people and things which had made me, and which I cared about. But in most cases there was no mistaking his lack of interest. At these times I wanted to shake him, to shout: 'Who are you? What do you want? Why aren't you like me?'

We both knew the answer to those questions, though. I was black, and I'd always be an immigrant, exiled from paradise, full of complex and contradictory loyalties. Half of him was white, and he'd grown up knowing he was an Englishman. The only bit of it which made any sense was that we loved each other.

The next moment the mood would pass and I'd know that I had been in the grip of an irrational and destructive passion.

On the way down to Maman's house I told him about her. I'd told him some it on the occasion of our last visit, but then he'd been younger and I'd left out a lot. This time I was leaving things out again. Not so much perhaps, but I still wasn't ready to tell him everything I remembered.

Maman Nightingale was from one of the islands where they spoke a French dialect and, together with half a dozen other local black boys, I was crazy about her daughter Francine. We hung around their house most days tripping over our tongues. But instead of throwing us out Maman treated us with a kind of amused affection, and as time went on most of us hung out at Maman's as much for the food and the company as for a chance of squeezing up Francine. She cooked the same food she used to back home in the Caribbean – pepperpot, black puddings, exotic bakes – there was always a pot on the fire, and if you were one of her boys, as she called us, you could always walk in and pull up a chair and have a meal. For many of us it was like a second home.

'What happened to Francine, Dad?'

'Oh, she got married to some guy none of us knew.'

He'd been a drummer with a reggae group that appeared on *Top of the Pops* a couple of times, and one day she'd turned up pregnant. Now Francine was a middle-aged matron whose youngest child was older than my son. There was no more to say about her, and I couldn't think of any words to explain how a lady older and fatter than his mum had once been the most mysterious and exciting creature in the universe.

Nothing seemed to have changed at Maman's house. She led us down the hall with her huge arm tucked firmly through my son's and sat him at the big round table. There were already four small boys sitting there eating, and Maman waved at them grandly.

'My grandsons.'

'Francine's?'

'No. No,' she said. 'She only has girls. These are my sons' children.'

She had four sons, three of them older than her daughter, but the last one, Aubrey, had been born about the same time as Francine's first.

My son, who avoided unfamiliar dishes, didn't like Caribbean food, and hated fish, picked politely at the mess of shrimps and aubergine in front of him. I headed Maman off before she could remark on his appetite.

'We had a big breakfast. He's not greedy like me.'

She accepted the excuse, but I had the suspicion that she was busy turning over the problem in her mind.

'I see they killed your friend Aston,' she said.

I grabbed at the subject with relief. My son had raised his eyebrows when I said what I did, and I was afraid that he was going to say straight out that he didn't like the food. He'd think that was being honest, if he thought about it, but Maman would find it rude – a painful insult.

'Yes. They still don't know who did it.'

'What happened?'

She was eager for details. Later on in the afternoon she'd be shopping down Harrow Road and by the time she got home she'd have passed on most of what I told her to a couple of dozen people.

I told her about the body, the sort of thing she'd have read in the papers. I told her too about the experience I'd had on the estate, dressing it up a bit, and she clicked her tongue with concern.

'You want Aubrey,' she said.

I certainly did.

'That's a good idea. But is he working?'

A look of disgust crossed her face.

'Working? Working what? He's at the gym, building himself

up so he can sit here and watch telly the rest of the day.'

The older Nightingale boys used to have a formidable local reputation before they declined into middle age, and in some ways Aubrey had surpassed them. He'd first got into trouble nicking out of shops and after that he'd grown up in and out of a series of residential homes. Along the way he'd acquired an expertise in the martial arts, backed up by the sort of physique which took several hours a day to develop and maintain. That's what he did in the mornings. In the afternoons he hung out. Sometimes he was arrested. He liked his life and he was good-natured and polite.

'He's a good boy,' I said. She always liked to hear that. 'He could work with me for a little while.'

Maman's expression took on an animated air. Perhaps this time Aubrey would get himself together.

'I'll tell him, as soon as he comes in.'

That was good enough. Aubrey would do what Maman told him, and with him watching my back I could stop worrying.

Back in the car the questions started.

'You didn't tell me this job was dangerous, Dad.'

'It's not really.'

'Why do you want Aubrey to go around with you then?'

'Just a precaution.'

'But, Dad. You're mad. Those guys don't mess about.'

He tried another tack.

'Why do you like that Maman so much?'

'She reminds me of home, and when I came here first.'

'Oh. The old days.'

He talked about those times that I'd told him about as if they were prehistoric.

'Something like that. It's like my mother. Family.'

'Granny? She's nothing like that. Well, a little bit. But nobody in our family talks like that.'

I looked at him sideways. He didn't understand, I thought, although he was trying to.

'She's always been poor. Nothing very good has ever happened to her, and likely never will, but she's worked hard and made other people happy and been happy herself, and I sort of admire that.'

'Ah.'

End of story. He didn't want to talk about it any more, and I couldn't think of anything else to say.

Chapter 14

After dropping my son off at home I stopped at Sophie's studio near Camden Town, but she was out. It was a sunny afternoon and the streets were crowded with shoppers, but I went through them absently, my mind struggling with the riddles of the last couple of days. A fair-haired woman went across the pedestrian crossing in front of the car, turning to give me a little smile as she did so. I thought about Kim. Where was she? What could I do to find her?

As I paused in the traffic across the High Street, a toothless drunk with scraggly tow-coloured hair falling over his face tapped on the window, holding out a cupped hand. He started shouting abuse when I ignored him and drove on, the round crusted mouth opening and closing on a black hole. In front of me the exhaust pipes turned the air a greyish blue. Camden Town.

My mood had improved by the time I got up to the small block of flats where Tommy lived. It had been renovated and converted specifically to suit the needs of the old people who liver there; a holiday camp for old women, Tommy called it. 'You wouldn't believe the things they get up to,' he'd say, his eyes rolling. 'You wouldn't believe.'

His flat was on the first floor. It was reached by walking through into a courtyard, then up the stairs. Two old ladies,

95

one black, one white, were blocking the way and I hovered politely till they moved aside.

'Who are you looking for?' the black woman asked me.

'Tommy. Is he in?'

The two women looked at each other, eyebrows raised.

'Oh yes,' the black one said. 'He's in. Go on up.'

I smiled and nodded my thanks and went on up, but I'd only got about halfway when the sound of the old man's voice stopped me.

'You. You boy.'

I looked up, and he was standing above me on the landing, his face contorted with anger, his eyes narrowed to tiny red slits, his stubbly grey jaw trembling.

'You. Yes. You.'

I grinned at him and spread my hands wide. He was dressed in a singlet under which his huge belly bulged and strained, but it showed off his arms, still massive and muscular. He must have been pushing seventy, but he looked hale and hearty as if he was just about to go off and stoke a boiler or raise an anchor, which was pretty funny, considering that Tommy had spent his entire sea-going career as a steward on board various passenger ships.

'Tommy. It's nice to see you.'

'Boy. Don't give me nice,' he shouted. 'I don't want to hear nice. I thought I was going to have to come and give you a good beating to get you here.'

This could go on for ever, so I ran up the rest of the stairs and put my arms round him. He grinned widely and hugged me. He'd always had the widest, happiest grin of anyone I knew, but this time there were tears in his eyes.

'Tommy. Tommy,' I said. In a minute we'd both be bawling.

As if he sensed the danger, Tommy pulled away from me.

'Come inside. Come inside, you damn dog,' he said in a low voice. He put his head close to mine as we went.

'You see those two old bitches down there? Tonight, tonight, they dead from curiosity.' He laughed, as if the prospect cheered him up.

His sitting room was the same as I remembered it. A square shape, with cream-painted walls, a big sofa, telly, the rest of it choked with small ornaments, animals, ashtrays, plates, in brass and silver. Tommy's chair was a big leather monster lined with cushions.

The room smelled of rum, and Tommy poured me a glass from the bottle beside him without asking if I wanted it. When he set it down I picked the bottle up to look at the brand. It was one that I vaguely remembered from my childhood, but I knew that they didn't export it.

Tommy anticipated the question. He waggled his finger.

'I still have friends. They bring this for me.'

Get him started on the smuggling in which he'd been involved, and he'd go on four hours.

'I can't drink the piss they sell here and call it rum.'

Like all connoisseurs of the liquor he was outraged by the ugly fortified taste of the brew you got in Britain when you asked for rum.

I nodded and murmured my agreement, and my eye caught the photograph lying beside his chair. He saw me looking and handed it to me. I recognised it right away. I'd seen it dozens of times, but the way that Tommy looked at me when he reached across, made me look at it seriously, as if for the first time.

It was an old snapshot, going yellowish-brown with age and handling. It showed Tommy standing in the middle of the village street where I'd been born, flanked by a little group of boys. Aston and I were there, grinning self-consciously into the camera. Tommy was dressed in a white suit and white shoes, topped off by a broad-brimmed white hat. There was a tough, good-looking face under the hat. I could never remember having the picture taken, although Aston said he did. I did remember, though, that we thought Tommy looked like a star.

He'd been sitting there, I thought, looking at that picture.

'So it took the dead,' Tommy said, 'to get you here.'

The way he used the word gave the corpse a new kind of existence. A formal identity. That was the way they said it when I was a child. The dead is coming.

I made an apologetic face. Another difference between me and Aston. I couldn't imagine how he found the time and energy to keep up all his relationships.

'Who killed him, Tommy?'

'I don't know. It wasn't the little boy. He used to be there all the time. He respected Aston.'

Respect wasn't a word he used lightly. It had something to do with loyalty and love as well.

'Suppose something happened to turn his respect into hate? With a knife it doesn't take much. One jook. Bam. It's too late.'

Tommy brooded.

'I know what was going on. Suzie told me about it. Maybe at the spur of the moment the boy could have done something. But he wouldn't run and hide. Make a mystery of it.'

'You think Suzie's telling us everything?'

'Of course.' He sounded indignant. 'She's a good girl. When I went there first I kept my eye on her, and if she was in any way funny I wouldn't have gone back. I don't let white people scorn me. But she was okay.'

I considered Tommy's self-righteous expression. He used to call Suzie his daughter-in-law, and when he'd had a couple of drinks he used to try and feel her up. On special occasions, his birthday, Christmas, she'd get on his knee with an indulgent air. Poor old sod, she'd say, not much in his life. Tommy probably loved Suzie as much as he did Aston. Or more.

'You're barking up the wrong tree, boy. Why don't you check out the baby mother?'

I sat up with a jerk.

'What? The baby mother?'

Tommy smiled grimly.

'He came here. The middle of the night last week. She just told him. He was thinking over the situation. I told him. Don't take no pressure. Let them do what they like.'

'Who are we talking about?'

'The little girl, man. Whashename. Kim. Aston hand it some licks. He was a dangerous cocksman.'

He sounded admiring, and I nearly said that we hadn't understood the danger of what Aston was doing, but something about Tommy's face told me to shut up.

'He brought her here a couple of times at the beginning. She had some trouble with the parents and Aston was helping her. She was nice. Hello Tommy this and hello Tommy that. But I wasn't too interested. I told Aston. That's jailbait.'

'What kind of trouble with the parents?'

'I don't really know. Maybe like the father used to beat her too bad or something. I don't know.'

'The parents knew about the baby?'

'That was the whole trouble. They wanted to send her away somewhere. Something like that. I told him. Let them do what they want.'

His voice was developing a querulous, grumbling tone. He was getting tired.

'So that was it,' I said. 'What do you think happened?'

'Wait nuh?' This was irritable. 'That wasn't all. This father. Aston had found out something. The father was a crook. They had some kind of wickedness going in the town hall. Aston had something on him and he said he was going to use it to blow them all away. He didn't tell me what it was, but he was laughing. He had him by the balls, he said. By the balls.'

'You're sure he didn't tell you what it was about.'

'You think because I old I stupid? He said a lot of things but he used to keep that kind of business to himself. He used to talk over what he was going to do but he didn't tell me the details. I know it was a whole gang of them. The father, the uncle and some more.'

'You think that was what it was all about?'

'I don't know. If I was younger I would go and sort it out, but I have to leave it to you. That's why I'm giving you this information. You understand me?'

He sat up straight and glared at me. I nodded and looked straight back at him.

'Don't worry, Tommy. I'll find out. I promise you.'

He grunted and turned away to pour himself another glass.

This time he didn't pour one for me. It was a signal that he wanted to be alone, and I wondered whether he was wishing that I was the dead, instead of his beloved Aston. He probably was, I thought.

'Tommy,' I said. 'Look after yourself. I'll see you soon.'

'In another twenty years,' he grumbled. But the next moment he looked up, smiled his big smile and held out his hand. I shook it, holding it tight, then let him go and went on out the door.

As I came to the bottom of the stairs, the door of the flat below Tommy's opened and the old white woman I'd seen before came out and spoke to me.

'How is he?'

'Fine.'

'His friend passed away suddenly you know. Councillor Edwards. He used to come here all the time. Tommy's taking it badly.'

'I know,' I said. 'Keep an eye on him, won't you?'

'Oh. We will,' she said earnestly.

I went away smiling. If they irritated Tommy enough, maybe he'd forget about Aston for a while. But perhaps I was wrong about that. If the old ladies cared about him, it was probably mutual, and instead of being a nuisance, they'd be sharing what he felt. That was how I hoped it was anyway.

Chapter 15

The evening was dwindling into the dark side of twilight when I left Tommy's place, and going past the queue outside one of the cinemas it struck me that it was Saturday night. The going-steady crowd would be out in force, holding hands and walking with their arms around each other. Teenage fashions changed all the time, but that stuff was for ever. I laughed cynically at the thought, but somehow the car began taking the turnings that would lead down to Camden Town, where Sophie lived.

The lights were on in the studio which meant that she was there.

The flat was on top of a rambling block near Primrose Hill, purpose built by a Housing Association with a group of studios at the top, four storeys up. She'd taken the place over from an illustrator who'd struck it big and moved to the USA. She thought of it as a good omen, and she'd been happy there, going round the flats, getting the children to pose for her and carry her equipment, a familiar sight, one of the artistic community. In spite of her contempt for the small scale and the cosiness of the country, this sense of belonging was important to her.

I ran up the steps and banged on the door. We had keys to each other's flats, but we had an agreement not to use them except in emergencies.

She opened the door after what seemed like a long while. When she saw me, she smiled, gave me a quick peck on the cheek, and turned back into the flat.

'Come in.'

I followed her in through the tiny hallway formed by the corridor between the bathroom and the kitchen. It gave out on to a big room, the width of the flat, faced by a line of windows running from waist level up to the ceiling, half of which consisted of slanting panes of glass rising to a peak. The place offered a view of the London sky which was absorbing, a constant moving show, even on the darkest nights.

On this occasion, though, my attention was riveted on the man who was standing by the long trestle table which stood in the middle of the room. He'd been leafing through a pile of photos and when he looked up I saw a smooth tanned face, straight dark brown hair cut short, a moustache turned down at the ends, and lustrous brown eyes. He was wearing a light oatmeal suit with a neat striped tie, and he looked like one of the South Americans I'd seen photographed playing polo or standing around in hotel lounges.

She introduced us casually, his name was Osvaldo Martín, and he came forward in two steps to shake hands with a little ducking bow of the head. There was something military about his bearing and I half expected him to click his heels. We made conversation while Sophie made coffee.

They had met a long time ago in the USA, she shouted from the kitchen, and she'd been staggered, when she was up at some air base in the Midlands taking pix of pilots for a woman's mag – they were supposed to be hunks or something – and this guy had taken off his helmet and it was Osvaldo. He was training on jets now, and he had only been in England a few weeks.

'Can you believe that?' she said, appearing with some cups.

Osvaldo smiled at me, twisted his mouth, shrugged and made a quizzical gesture with his hands.

'Small world,' he said.

I agreed. He had an accent which I recognised as Venezuelan, but the style and rhythm of his English was American Ivy League. When I told him where I came from he said he'd been there. He'd been part of a helicopter rescue team which had toured the region in an exchange programme, and he told me about the changes in the look of the place which had occurred recently. He talked well, he was charming and knowledgeable and very smart, and by the time he said he had to go I would have needed very little encouragement to hate his guts.

Sophie saw him to the door. They said goodbye speaking in rapid Spanish and I heard the sound of a kiss. It gave me a sinking feeling, but I kept on staring out of the window.

The sky was growing darker, a deep violet stain spreading over it, except for one small patch in the bottom right-hand corner which was a dull, dirty grey streaked with orange. I wondered for a moment whether it was a good sign or a bad one. On the whole I thought it must be bad, and I resolved not to ask her about her relationship with Martín.

She came back laughing, in a high good humour, but I couldn't tell whether or not that was put on for my benefit. I began telling her about Tommy and she listened attentively, laughing at the funny bits. Encouraged, I told her about the party and my fight with the women, hamming it up to make her laugh some more.

Afterwards she took a package out of the freezer and put it in the microwave oven. She wasn't a good cook and putting one of these prepared meals in the microwave was as far as she was ready to go. We ate at the end of the long table after she'd cleared a space by pushing aside the sheets of paper and the light box which occupied it.

Halfway through the meal she stared at me intently.

'You have to find this girl. She must know what was going on.'

I made a face at her.

'I agree. The problem is how to find her. She could be anywhere.'

'You're not thinking,' she said. 'She's well brought up. Everyone's been protecting her or telling her what to do. She told

Aston, she told her parents. She wouldn't just run off, and if her parents were going to send her away they wouldn't give her a ticket and say go. She'd be with a relative. Not even an old friend. A relative. In the circumstances almost certainly a woman. Almost certainly a relative of her mother's. Grandmother, sister. Find them and she'll be there. Trust me. It's the sort of thing that's obvious to a woman.'

I laughed, but what she said had convinced me. After we'd finished, I rang Walter.

'Bloody hell,' he said, 'it's nearly midnight on Saturday, what's the matter with you?'

Sophie was clearing away the dishes, and I watched her as she moved. Tonight she was wearing a long skirt with buttons down the front. Only two of them were fastened and, as she moved, I could see every inch of her long thighs. I wondered whether Osvaldo had looked at her in the same way. I turned my back on her and told Walter what Tommy had said about the Parkers. I left out the bit about Kim, but even so he gave me a long, thoughtful silence before he answered.

'I don't know,' he said. 'Are you sure the old git's got it right?'

'I'm sure,' I said. 'He knows exactly what he's on about.'

His way of referring to Tommy made me a bit touchy. Walter's father had split when he was a child, and I knew that he viewed all black men that age with hostility.

'He mentioned an uncle,' I said. 'Who's that?'

'Frank. Frank Connor. He's kind of a supplier. Works with Keith for us. He's nobody. His firm's totally dependent on the business Parker gives him. And he's a drunk. I'd leave them alone.'

'Come on. This is the most interesting thing that's come up in the whole business.'

'Sammy,' he said. 'I don't know what you're doing. You're supposed to be writing something about Aston and his politics. Something about the problems of black politicians. What's this investigation shit?'

'Hey. Hold it. Hold it,' I told him. 'If I do this I'll do it my way. This is my business, you know what I mean?'

I heard him sighing.

'I don't want to have this conversation right now,' he said. 'Can we meet tomorrow?'

'Sure.'

He named the time and place and put the phone down.

While we were talking Sophie had handed me a glass of brandy and now I went to sit beside her facing the windows. It was a dark night with a mass of black cloud chasing quickly across the sky. The stars kept showing out then disappearing. She'd left one small lamp on in the corner, and the room was cloaked in a comfortable shadow.

'He's trying to use you,' she said.

'Sure he is,' I said. 'He's a politician. That's how they are.'

Sometimes her way of stating the obvious got up my nose. The other thing, of course, was Osvaldo Martín. I hadn't asked her about him, and she hadn't volunteered anything further. But he was still at the back of my mind. I felt her noting my spikiness.

'I had an idea,' she said. 'The woman Spid. Maybe I can go and photograph her. Perhaps she'll tell me something.'

'What makes you think she'll talk to you at all? She's kind of paranoiac about the press. I don't blame her, but it doesn't make things easy.'

She thought about it.

'When I took those photographs I promised to send her some prints. I was busy so I never did. I could get in touch with her and ask her to do some more. For my exhibition.'

'What exhibition?'

'London Women. I told you about it.'

I'd forgotten. She was doing pictures for a show at a local arts centre with a group of women photographers. The way that she and her colleagues moved between art and commerce was about the only thing that interested me about her work.

'It's the sort of thing that she'd respond to. She might even know about it.'

She was right, but I felt an intense reluctance about her being involved in whatever was going on.

'If you don't want me involved in your business,' she said, 'it's okay.'

The phrase struck echoes. It was what Tommy or perhaps my father would say. Don't get women involved in your business.

'No. Come off it,' I said. 'It's a good idea. Thanks.'

I turned and kissed her. She put her arms around my neck and relaxed against me. I could feel her big, firm breasts moving against my chest. At the end of this horrible week, I thought, here is the prize. I put my hand between her smooth cool thighs, and she squeezed me tighter, but in a moment she took her mouth away from mine and whispered in my ear.

'I have to work. In the dark room.'

That was the kitchen.

'Oh bugger it,' I said.

She laughed and pulled away from me.

'You go to bed,' she said. 'I'll join you later.'

Later on I'd be asleep, and her work could take all night.

The bed was on a raised platform someone had built her at the back of the room. Underneath was the desk where she worked occasionally. On top of the platform, just below the ceiling, it felt like another little room, private and isolated. On a good night you could lie there for ever, looking out at the changing sky.

It wasn't a good night. She went into the kitchen and came back out to tell me that she'd arranged a shoot at Camden Lock next morning. It was the only day she could do it, because of the market, but there would be time for us to hang out a bit before she went. I didn't reply and in a moment she sprang up the steps, jumped on to the bed, rolled on top of me and hugged and kissed me fiercely. But in another minute she had rolled away and jumped down.

When I heard her go into the kitchen and fix the door shut, I climbed down to get myself a book. I was looking for something light and amusing. Perhaps a tough thriller, but it wasn't the sort of thing she read. Most of her books were about politics or photography, and eventually I picked up a paperback anthology of poems.

Back in bed I read Robert Frost slowly, remembering when I'd first read him in the school library, a quiet place which the nutters mostly avoided, and where I spent my lunch breaks.

'One could do worse than be a swinger of birches,' I muttered to myself, and then I was asleep.

Chapter 16

When I woke next morning the sky was growing pale with the promise of an early sun. It was still dark and shadowy in the flat and I knew I wouldn't get back to sleep, so I climbed carefully over Sophie and went down the ladder. She hadn't moved, but to avoid waking her I dressed quietly in the dim light, picked up her keys from where she usually left them on the table and tiptoed out.

It was only a short step to Primrose Hill and I hurried to try and get there before sunrise. At that hour the birds were making a racket, and I sat on a bench for a while listening to them and watching the sun, veiled in scraps of cloud and mist, heave itself laboriously over the houses. Afterwards I walked down the hill and made my way slowly back towards Sophie's flat.

All this time I thought about what was going on between the two of us. There were several things I would have liked to say to her but all of them sounded like some kind of complaint, and I knew from experience that complaining wasn't the way to resolve the alienation and distance I was feeling.

The problem was that in a year or so she'd changed considerably from the person I'd met. Then, we seemed to have a lot in common. One of the things we talked about, for instance, was how it felt to be what she called properly black. She said her mother had African blood, 'maybe half, less maybe.'

'Imagine,' she'd said. 'We never talked to each other about it. That's how it is in Latin America. If you're a musician or an artist or an anthropologist, something like that, you can talk about African heritage. To talk about being black. Impossible.'

In the USA and later in Britain she'd gone through a kind of trauma when she met people whose skin was as light as hers and who called themselves black. Such experiences fascinated her and she talked about them frequently. Then, all of a sudden, she stopped.

I hadn't noticed at first. What I noticed was that her hair had begun to wave rather than curl, and instead of becoming more English as I'd expected, she seemed more Latin than ever. A trace of the accent she had lost crept back into her speech, and she would shout across the street in Spanish to her friends. *'Mujer. Mujer. Mira.'*

As I got out of the park and into the street, I saw the first person I'd encountered so far. She wore a dressing gown with a long nightie and slippers below it, a scarf over her head, and she was being towed along by a pair of vicious-looking Dobermanns. I speeded up and crossed the road to avoid the little procession. When I looked back she was at the park gates, bending over to release the dogs. They squatted in the middle of the path, defecated carefully, then went tearing up the hill. The woman loitered behind them, smiling indulgently. Owning a pair of Dobermanns probably meant never having to say sorry.

I turned the corner, losing sight of them, and went back to my own demons. The trouble with my reasoning, I thought, was that its purpose was to divert me from the real problem. So what if she'd changed? I could be kidding myself about that anyway. Perhaps the only change was that she no longer fancied me. *No hay problema.*

Back in the flat she was still asleep, and it was a few hours before she came down the steps. In the meantime I'd had a shower, read the Sunday papers, drunk three cups of tea, and dozed off again. When I woke up I could hear her splashing in the bathroom and I went to make some coffee. The thoughts of the morning seemed like a dream, the details of which had faded, leaving footprints of depression on the nerves.

She came out, damp, smelling like a tangerine, and waving a hair dryer around. Suddenly she was full of hustling animation, moving round the flat with the speed and unpredictability of a butterfly, shouting above the buzz of the dryer and stacking bits of equipment.

Half an hour later I was on my way up to North London to meet Walter. Past the old Harringay stadium the traffic slowed down and I braked to avoid a little group of children crossing against the lights. The street had become an avenue of shops, Greeks and Indians, open for business and trading furiously. Aubergines and big peppers; vegetables as far as the eye could see. The colour and bustle of a festival.

I'd seen it like this dozens of times before, but the sight always did something to me. When I lived there as a boy Sunday used to be drab and grey, nothing to do till the pictures started in the evening. My memories were of a different place.

At the other end of the street I parked by the side of the common, walked across the grass and sat next to Walter on a bench facing the cinema opposite.

'See that cinema?' I said. 'The last thing I saw there was *Point Blank* with Lee Marvin. He was a guy named Walker, trying to get back some money the Mafia did him out of. I want my money, he said. Give me my money.'

'How long ago was that?'

I shrugged.

'Before your time.'

Walter laughed.

'You know something,' he said. 'You're a survivor. I used to admire that, but it's like you died years ago, and now you're like a ghost, a bundle of memories and frustrated desires haunting the city.'

'Jeez, Walter,' I said. 'You're always surprising me. You're so smart.'

'I don't know,' he said. 'Maybe this wasn't such a great idea after all. You've upset Parker. Got right up his nose.'

'So?'

'Listen Sammy, the guy's important. You know what makes it all run? It's not these people.'

He gestured at the shoppers. On the other side of the railings three Indian women stalked past, their trousers billowing, the tight cuffs showing off their delicate ankles. They didn't look at us, not even the flash of an eye. Behind them tottered two little girls, dressed in exactly the same way, looking like miniature copies of their mums.

'It's not elections,' Walter said. 'When you get up there you think about your friends and your enemies. Your friends help you make things happen. Your enemies stop you. Who's on our side? There's the left, the gays, the greens, the freaks, Troops Out, anti apartheid and that. Then there's the liberal middle class, the polytechnic lecturers and their chums, but they're not important except for numbers. They don't have opinions. Just preferences. Then there's the spoilers. The lefties who come out of the little revolutionary groups and join a big party to make mischief, because they think parliamentary democracy is a con and needs exposing. Turn your back on them and they rip your ass to shreds.'

He stopped, looking around and thinking about it.

'But then you come to the old white working class. They're not liberal but they're still central in the trade unions, the works department, things like that. And they built the Labour Club. They only just let us in. Don't get me wrong. They can't run things the way they used to twenty years ago. Not in London. They need us. They need our votes. That's why I'm here. But they've been doing their own thing going back years. We balance them, and just because we've got a high profile around here everyone forgets how strong they are, but don't think they can't pull the plug because they can.'

'Parker's going to pull the plug because I said hello to his wife?'

Walter made a sound halfway between a moan and a sigh.

'He's not the only one. What about Spid? She's well on my back.'

He sighed again.

'I can cope with that, but Parker's bad news. He's the godfather. There's a whole family of them. Mostly Irish. The sort that came here centuries ago and dug in. Sparks, the councillor you talked to, he's one of them too, a cousin. Parker's dad was the big noise around here once. He had it all. Local contractor, Freemason, councillor, the lot. He didn't employ blacks. Made no secret of it. He was one of those not-in-my-lifetime guys. Blacks would sit on the council one day, but not in my lifetime. If you didn't like it he'd stamp on you. Aston said they used to beat the shit out of people right there in front of the Labour Club. The way things are today, being in the same party as people like us would probably have killed him. That's Parker's background and he expected to inherit. But all of a sudden everything's changed. Parker's one of those who've never accepted it. So it's one long struggle with that crowd. They don't want the things we want and if they don't want anything to happen you have to fight them. You understand me. You have to pick your issues all the time, and this.'

He raised his hands and let them fall. 'We've got more important issues to fight.'

'So Parker says jump and you jump.'

'It's not like that,' he said angrily. He stood up, spun around, faced me again and pointed his finger. 'One day soon we're going to smash the lot of them.'

I looked at him without speaking and he calmed down and sat on the bench again.

'Look, Sammy,' he said. 'When I came to see you about this I thought you'd do us a bit of good, give us a boost, but the way you go about things is just giving me hassle. I mean I'm not trying to tell you what to write. I wouldn't try to do that. You're the governor, man. Just write the bloody thing and stop pissing about upsetting people.'

Our eyes met.

'I told you before,' I said. 'You may take your orders from Parker and that lot, but I don't. All this is about Aston. Kid I grew up with long ago and far away. I'll upset who I like.'

He looked away.

'All right, Sammy. You do what you like, but don't come to me for anything.'

He got up and started walking towards the street.

'Message received,' I said, but he was already several paces away and I don't think he heard me.

Chapter 17

'I'm going into the garden with Sammy, Mum,' Suzanne said.

Helen looked up. She had the same eyes as her daughter and a frosty way of aiming them which made it seem as if she was assessing you and coming to a stern conclusion. With her iron-grey hair and cool manner she appeared at first sight to be a formidable person, and I was certain the way she acted was an indication that she disliked me intensely. Later on, when it was clear that we got on well, I realised that her manner towards people she loved was only slightly warmer.

'Yes,' she said. For a long moment she looked at us without expression, then went back to her book. Suzie rolled her eyes in exasperation and led the way out of the back door. She thought her mother was cold and picky, and sometimes everything Helen did annoyed her. It was one of the things about which we used to disagree.

I had gone home for a change of clothes after seeing Walter, then driven back to the house, arriving in time for a late lunch with Suzie and Helen. Her father had heart trouble and he'd gone home by train in case the strain was too much for him. At the table we didn't talk about Aston. Instead Helen held forth angrily about religious fundamentalism. She had passionately radical views, and a contempt bordering on fanaticism for most of the pillars of established society. This new oppression, however, drew from her a rage she'd never wasted on the Archbishop of Canterbury.

I listened to her with a kind of delight. She'd been too late for the suffragettes and too early for feminism, but her radicalism was so English, so characteristic of a familiar liberal and professional type, that it made her anger lovable and her vitriolic explosions endearing.

Afterwards, when she went out to make coffee, I asked Suzie about the Parkers. I couldn't be sure whether I would have told her about Kim if we'd been alone, but with Helen in the house it was impossible. As it was, she gave me an odd look when I mentioned Keith Parker.

'Later,' she said. 'Let's talk about it later.'

In the garden she was still fuming mildly about her mother.

'She's so bossy,' she said. 'Always telling other people what to think.'

It was odd, hearing a woman in her thirties use those words about her mother, but I supposed that was part of the problem.

'Oh well,' I said when she seemed to be running out of steam. 'What about this guy Parker?'

She thought for a moment. Then she told me more or less what I already knew about him, which was what I expected.

'Someone mentioned a brother. Frank Connor?'

'Yes. Frank Connor. Shelagh's brother. Bit of a creep. He's not like Keith. Keith is a total shit but he's got some character, whereas Frank, if it wasn't for Marcie he'd probably be pushing a wheelbarrow. Keith keeps him going, probably for Shelagh's sake. He worked for Old Man Parker. Thought the sun shone out of the old creep's bottom. But that's how they are. Everyone knows old Parker was a racist pig, and then they go on about the good old days when he was around. It's telling you something.'

'Who's Marcie?'

She flicked her eyes sideways at me and laughed.

'Frank's wife. You haven't met old Marcie yet. That will be a treat. She's a real piece of work. But why do you want to know? What's going on?'

I hesitated, but it was obvious that I had to tell her some version of the truth.

'I was trying to reach Kim. She's gone off somewhere and I thought maybe the uncle and aunt.'

'Why Kim?'

I told her that it was because Kim had worked for Aston and she might tell me useful things about him and what he was doing. She made an impatient sound.

'You don't have to sound so embarrassed. I can make a good guess why you're humming and hawing over this, and it wouldn't surprise me to know that Aston was screwing the tight little pants off her. She used to moon about after him making goo goo eyes, and he wasn't exactly Mister Self Control. So what's it all about?'

'You probably know as much about it as I do,' I said. A bit stiffly.

'Come on, Sammy. I'm not exactly the good little wifey next door. I knew the man.'

Her voice broke, and she put her face to her hands.

'Don't get me started,' she said. 'I don't want her to see me standing in the garden crying.'

I got between her and the windows and we stood there in silence for a moment. She sniffed, blew her nose and wiped her eyes.

'Marcie works at the town hall,' she said. 'Did you know that? She's in housing. But I can tell you where to find them tonight probably.'

'Where?'

'The Labour Club. Have you been there?'

She told me where it was.

'Keith's father built it. Well not exactly built. It's a big house some factory owner built before the First World War when people could still remember this being a small town just outside London. The party bought it after the last war and did it up. Keith's father was in a small way then, but he got the job. The old wretch died in the sixties, but there's a big painting of him in the bar downstairs. Keith shows it to everyone. Working class family tradition and all that balls. It's a terrible painting, but Keith wouldn't know.'

'He won't show it to me,' I said.

She gave me a curious look and I told her about my clash with Keith and about my conversation with Walter.

She frowned.

'He's probably scared.'

'Who, Walter?'

'No. Walter's doing his job. He probably feels threatened. He'll be under a lot of pressure from all sides. No. I was talking about Keith.'

She looked around as if by reflex.

'I don't suppose it matters now. I was sworn to secrecy, but whatever it was between Aston and Kim started when he was doing his big brother act. He was driving home late one night and he saw her car standing near the park with the door open. The lights were on and it looked sort of peculiar. He recognised the car. So he got out and found her standing by the railings crying. It turned out that Keith had given Shelagh a walloping, and that was something he did quite often. He likes to use his fists. He's never got into any trouble, but he's been in quite a few brawls. In pubs. On the street. That kind of thing. And paranoiac. Accuses her of sleeping with the milkman. Stuff like that. He won't want strangers talking to her.'

Shelagh's face behind the dark glasses flashed through my mind.

'Old Tommy said that Aston was all excited about something he had on Keith. Do you think that was it?'

'It's not likely. Aston's known about all this for ages. By the way, if you meet her take care with Marcie. She's bad.'

'What do you mean?'

She hesitated. I thought for a moment that she wasn't going to answer. Then she started.

'That woman gave me some of the worst moments of my life. The stupid thing is that it was all about the job. She worked her way up in housing. When she married Frank it didn't exactly hurt her prospects, because of the family connection. Keith did most of the work that Direct Labour couldn't do and anyway the same mafia had been running the town hall for years. Well, a few years ago she became the Director's assistant. George Starkey. Towards the end he was chronically ill. Hanging on for retirement, and Marcie practically ran the show. Then he died and they appointed someone else, whose wife promptly took sick and he had to leave. Then there was a gap during which Marcie filled in again. Then they appointed a star.'

She laughed and named a man who had fought the last election for the Liberals.

'He was too busy, of course, to do much. Then he left. When they advertised again Marcie applied. It shouldn't have happened like that in the first place, and if Aston had been chair then it wouldn't have done. But in any case Marcie applied for the job. Some people thought she wasn't well enough qualified. Also there was her relationship with people like Keith, Frank and all that old contract gang. She really wanted it and she was really nice to everyone, especially Aston. Really, really, really nice, if you can believe her.'

Her tone was suddenly angry and bitter and she walked away from me towards the pear tree at the end of the garden. I followed her in silence, waiting for her to start again. She looked up, picked a green pear, looked at it, threw it away and dusted her hands.

'Well she didn't get the job. Oh, she was very good at running the office. A good bureaucrat; but they wanted more, and they appointed the present guy. The night after she heard she came round here. Aston wasn't in and I didn't know much about what had been happening. If I had I wouldn't have let her get started. But by the time I realised what she was up to, it was too late. She was suitably vicious. Told me a lot of things I didn't want to know. Couldn't shut her up.'

She stopped, reached out and played with the leaves on a drooping branch.

'It was the usual institutional gossip. You usually ignore it, but this was kind of —' she paused, looking for the right word — 'authentic. I took a week off and went home to mother. Then I got pissed off with the whole thing. Aston came up and we talked it over. It wasn't exactly all right, but we managed.'

I wondered what it had all been about. I could make a guess, but I could have been wrong. On the other hand, I didn't think it was the right time to pursue it. Suzanne looked straight at me. I'd been afraid she'd crack up again, but she didn't. Her lips were clamped tight and set in a stubborn, angry line.

'Poor Marcie,' she said. 'The funny thing is that, as a woman, I knew how she felt. A man who was that much of a scheming bitch would have impressed them. That was over six months ago. I haven't seen her since, but I suppose she's got over it.'

She gave a little laugh and shook her head.

'What a family.'

'What's Shelagh like?'

'She's nice. Living with that man's driven her round the bend of course, but I like her. She paints. The High Street. The park. Things like that. Local. She had some pictures in a show at the central library. Oh, a couple of years ago. But I haven't seen anything since. She's good-looking, intelligent, educated. More of everything her daughter is, but between the two of them they've driven her to drink.'

She glanced quickly at the house and I wondered whether she was thinking about Helen.

'She drinks?'

She shrugged.

'No more than the average desperate woman. He's proud of providing for her, so she's got nothing else to do. Sometimes it helps.'

'Can you get her to come and visit you? I'd like to meet her and chat to her.'

' I suppose I can.'

She stopped and stared at me. She grinned suddenly, a flash of the old Suze.

'Sammy Dean. What are you up to? Do you fancy Shelagh Parker?'

'Come off it, Suzie,' I said. 'This is business.'

But I said it without conviction and she didn't believe me.

Chapter 18

I phoned Aubrey before I went to the Labour Club that evening. I guessed that I would be on Parker's turf and I didn't want to be there on my own. Aubrey answered on the second ring and I asked him whether Maman had told him about the business in which I was engaged. He said she had. I told him that I wanted him that night and he said yes, I could pick him up. Then he put the phone down. He was a man of few words, but lots of words had never been necessary between us.

I'd sometimes been Maman's babysitter when Aubrey first arrived, and I'd taken him to kick his first football in the park. Later on, when he started getting into trouble, I'd been to court for him and bailed him out a couple of times. He hadn't grown up in the way I'd hoped, but I still liked him more than most people I knew, and I felt we cared about each other. He did errands and small jobs for me with an easy tolerance when he wasn't doing anything else, and, oddly, I thought that we gave each other confidence.

He was waiting for me by the door as I'd asked. If I went into the house it would take ages to get away from Maman. I saw her peeping through the front window all the same, and I waved.

'Aubrey,' I told him. 'You get bigger every time I see you.'

He acknowledged that with a complacent smile. His body

was one of his chief interests. He exercised with the compulsive dedication of an addict, and I knew that he studied himself with deep interest and pleasure. I didn't blame him. I was a six footer, but he was taller than me by two or three inches, with broad shoulders and slim hips. A man born to be noticed.

He got into the car, settled his long legs, and asked me where we were going. I told him and he nodded with a bored look but didn't comment.

I studied him out of the corner of my eye as I drove off. He was wearing a gold earring which he'd picked up during one of the periods when they'd locked him away in a residential home. There'd been a fashion for it then, and he'd come home, as Maman said, 'looking like a pirate'. I could see what she meant, because the earring gave his profile a dashing romantic air, a look which belied his placid temperament.

'Aubrey,' I said. 'Aren't you curious?'

He looked at me and grinned.

'You're always asking me that,' he said. 'Let me ask you something. You know what you're doing?'

I hesitated.

'Yeah. I think so.'

'Okay.'

We ran on up to North London without much conversation. When we went past Finsbury Park I told him how I used to hang out there with my schoolmates, trying to look up girls' dresses. He laughed out loud at that.

'Not something you did?'

He laughed again.

'No. That was the old days. It's different now.'

I'd heard something like that before from my son. But at the age of ten Aubrey was a lookout for a gang of steamers, and he'd worked his way up from there through TDA and B&E. My own schooldays seemed impossibly innocent in comparison.

The Labour Club was tucked away on the corner of a back street behind a big shopping mall, about half a mile from the civic centre. It was a rambling, bow-windowed, three-storeyed structure, standing detached behind a tall yew hedge that guarded a front garden, which was impressive for the area and consisted of a patchy lawn bordered by an old oak, two horse chestnuts and a few birches.

We parked on the street and went up the semi-circular driveway into the house. The door was open and led almost directly into a big barroom that looked like a comfortable pub.

Considering the size of the place, there was only a sprinkling of people present. Mostly white. About a quarter of them women, mostly middle-aged. Only four or five blacks and one Asian playing darts with a noisy group of men in their shirtsleeves. Over in the corner, in a little group of comfortable armchairs, were a woman and three men wearing suits and looking a little more prosperous and well set up than most of the others. They wouldn't have been out of place in the Conservative Club down the road.

We got one or two curious glances as we walked in, but we must have seemed a more or less badly matched pair. Aubrey was wearing 501s and a sleeveless pullover, showing off his biceps, and even with his smiling air and calm demeanour, he looked like the bad boy that he was. I was wearing a Féraud jacket with a red silk handkerchief flopping out the display pocket.

Neither of us looked much like party functionaries.

The man behind the bar was short and plump with rimless glasses and sandy hair, like a Hollywood character actor playing a bank clerk. He gave me the raised eyebrows, and I ordered a whisky for myself and an orange squash for Aubrey, who thought alcohol was a diabolical device for screwing up men's bodies and never touched it. If he was going to do that, he said, he might as well mess himself up with steroids, and that could never be, man.

I'd borrowed a party card earlier on, and I was ready to flash the red rose at the barman, but he didn't ask.

'I haven't been here a long time,' I said, when he came back with the drinks. I leaned confidentially on the bar. 'Is that Frank and Marcie Connor over there?'

I had a description from Suzanne, but I wanted to make sure.

I nodded at the little group sitting in the corner and, as I did so, Marcie looked up. It would have been impossible for her to have heard me at that distance and with so many other people buzzing away in the background, but she must have sensed we were talking about her, because she didn't look away.

'Go and play the machine,' I told Aubrey. 'I'm going to talk to these friends for a bit.'

There was an electronic games machine in the corner, and after I'd given him some money Aubrey sauntered over to it.

I strolled towards the Connors. I didn't know what I would say or do, but I guessed that stirring the pot couldn't lose me much. When she saw me coming Marcie said something to her companions and they turned to look at me. For a moment it had the same freezing quality as being on stage but I took a deep breath and charged on up the hill.

'Evening,' I said. 'Mind if I join you?'

Marcie grinned and looked slyly round the table at her friends.

'Are you a new member?' she asked me.

'No. My name's Sam Dean. I'm doing some writing for Walter Davis about Aston, and I have to talk to his friends and the people who worked with him.'

'Walter Davis?'

She had green eyes which, when she looked at me, seemed to stare with a surprising fixity, as if she was trying to read my mind. Her hair was black, bobbed short at the back, and her lipstick was bright red. In between all this colour her face looked white and pale.

'Yes,' I said firmly. 'I've been working with him.'

Walter will probably kill me, I thought, but I might as well be hung for a sheep.

'Well,' said one of the men, 'we'll leave you to it.'

He stood up. So did one of the other men. They both wore grey suits and had curly hair and pink, scraped-looking faces. I guessed the one that didn't get up was Frank.

'Just a minute,' Marcie said to me. 'Sit down.'

I sat down and she got up to talk to the men, standing a

little taller than I'd expected. She had her back to me and she was wearing a tight-fitting knee-length skirt with a long slit. When she moved the slit stretched and widened to show more of her long shapely legs. From where I sat I had a close-up view, and I stared, fascinated, until I heard a small sound, and I realised that Frank's eyes were on me. To cover my confusion I picked up my drink, swirled it round and took a swallow.

They were talking in low voices, obviously not for me, but I overheard one of the men say that he had to be in Wembley by nine and the rest of the conversation seemed to be about an arrangement to meet during the week. They left quickly without looking at me again and Marcie sat down.

'So what can I tell you?'

Frank hadn't said a word so far, and I looked quickly at him, a little uncertain about how to handle the two of them together. I couldn't be sure now they were both sitting, but I guessed he was a little shorter than she was, with a glazed reddish complexion, blond hair going a little bald in front, and watery blue eyes that looked at me without expression.

'Get us a drink, love,' she said to him, before I could reply.

He got up and asked me what I wanted. I was right about his height and in contrast to her low firm tones he had a voice that was lighter than I would have expected.

'Well, it's nothing special,' I said, when he'd moved off. 'You work in housing and I wondered whether you could tell me something about his professional interests, what sort of projects he started, you know the kind of thing. Something to give us an idea of how effective he was and why.'

She pursed her lips into a red O, uncrossed and crossed her legs, and leaned back with a thoughtful air.

'Of course I only know about housing. He left us months ago,' she said, 'and he was active in a lot of other directions, but I'll tell you what I know.'

The green eyes looked a question. I nodded reassurance and she began telling me some of the things I'd heard before.

When Aston took over the chair he'd had a special interest in the plight of the poor and the elderly. He was an efficient chairman, who did his paperwork and was good on detail. He'd started out having some success in cutting the housing list, then, like other chairmen before him, had run into the quicksands of policy on the homeless. There'd been a few rows over that, she remembered.

Frank came back during this recital and put the glasses on the table. She was drinking Campari and when he moved it in front of her the glass rattled a little, threatening to tip over. Marcie moved quickly, putting both hands to it, and I saw the left one for the first time. It was missing three fingers and curled around the glass it looked like a damaged and mutilated claw.

She saw me looking, and although there was no apparent change in her manner, I had the sense she was a little angry or upset. With a movement that was relaxed, but too quick to be entirely casual, she put her left arm down so that the hand was out of sight.

At that point I realised that she had kept it hidden, except for that one slip. Over the next half hour, in spite of myself, I found my eyes being continually drawn to her left side. But the way she managed it put me in mind of a skilled and practised conjuring act. The hand seemed always to be thrust into the pocket of her jacket, or behind a fold of her skirt or beneath the table. You'd think that next moment you were going to see it, then it would be gone. The effect was a little depressing when I realised what was happening.

Suddenly, her mood seemed to change again. She shifted over and leaned towards me a little, smiling, her eyes warmer.

'I don't suppose you remember me,' she said.

I looked at her carefully, casting through my memory, but there was nothing. It was almost worrying. I couldn't believe I'd forgotten. She was in her late thirties I guessed. Perhaps she'd been in my year at university. She fidgeted a little under the scrutiny, then she giggled and made a comically exaggerated, preening gesture, putting her right hand up and turning her profile to me.

That was disconcerting. At first she'd had an air of slightly suspicious authority which made me wary. Now she was radiating flirtatious charm. It was like being with a different woman, and it put me off balance.

'Sorry. I can't,' I said.

She pouted.

'That's not terribly flattering. Mind you, it was over ten years ago. Aston had been elected for the first time, and you were writing an article about him. I was working in the office and he introduced us. My hair was longer then.'

'And a different colour,' Frank said.

She gave him a patient look.

'And a different colour. But it was a good article. What paper was it in, Frank?'

'The *Guardian*,' Frank said. 'She got in the picture.'

'I made sure I did,' Marcie said.

She pointed her finger at me abruptly.

'That reminds me. There was an article just a few weeks back about the Kitchener Avenue redevelopment. That was really Aston's project from beginning to end. You ought to read it. Walter should have a clipping somewhere.'

'I'll get it,' I said, 'but what did it say?'

'Well. There was some trouble about the budgets. Overspending. That's usual, but Aston thought it would be a good idea to get some favourable publicity going. It always helps. The development was really a conversion of some of the old housing down there in the Old Town ward. It had stood empty for years, and Aston put together a package of business support and public financing for a mixed housing development with priority going to the elderly and handicapped. The area had been going down since the fifties and Kitchener Avenue was just the beginning of a plan for regenerating the whole ward. It will happen too, now it's started, except poor old Aston won't be there to see it.'

She looked away from me, but I could see her expression change, like a mask slipping, and for a moment she looked angry and haunted. I was looking at her and I didn't see Frank get up, but the movement was so unsteady or agitated that he knocked over the glasses and the ashtray went flying on to the floor with a crash.

Marcie glared at him and said his name sharply.

'Sorry,' Frank said, picking up the ashtray. 'I'll just get them in.'

He walked away, swaying a little, and I wondered whether the colour of his face was to do with the amount he drank.

Marcie shrugged and made a gesture with her open hand.

'Everyone around here is upset,' she said. 'It was such a shock. You knew him a long time, didn't you?'

I told her how long it had been and about how we'd run into each other during our vacations that summer. My mind was racing as I talked. Given what Suzanne had told me, there must have been a lot more to her relations with Aston than I was getting but she was too much in control to give away anything she didn't want to.

Frank came back with the drinks. He'd brought a double whiskey for himself as well as a pint of the bitter he'd been drinking before. Jamieson, by the look and smell of it, and he downed most of it in one gulp.

'Cheers,' Marcie said.

She seemed to be trying to jockey us back into a convivial mood.

'I suppose your niece, Kim, must be pretty upset. She worked for him didn't she? How is she taking it?'

She smiled reflectively, but there was a sly tinge to it, as if she could tell I was trying to worm something about Kim out of her.

'I haven't seen her since,' she said. 'I think she's away. But you're probably right.'

I was going to ask her more about Kim when there was a small commotion near the entrance and she looked up, smiled and waved.

I looked round and saw Keith Parker.

'Ah,' I said involuntarily.

'What's the matter?'

Her smile was positively malicious, and suddenly I sensed

that she'd known before I sat down about what I was doing and Keith's reaction to me.

'Your brother-in-law,' I told her. 'He doesn't like me very much.'

She grinned.

'Don't worry about him. His bark's worse than his bite.'

'What the bloody hell are you doing here?' Parker said behind me.

'Talking to me,' Marcie said.

Her tone was arch and, I suspected, calculated to urge Keith into an even greater rage.

'Get out,' Parker hissed between his teeth.

I looked around.

'This is the Labour Club, isn't it? Not your house.'

'Never mind whose house,' he said loudly. 'You're not even a member. Piss off.'

Marcie was smiling, her eyes bright. I was sure she was enjoying the atmosphere of violence and anger Parker had brought with him.

'What's he done for God's sake, Keith?'

He ignored the question for a moment as if he hadn't heard her. Then he looked round.

'He barged into my house and upset Shelagh. Asking questions.'

'Well, I'm not Shelagh,' she said firmly, 'and he's asking me questions, and I don't mind. So calm down.'

He stared at her and she looked back, calmly and intently. It was as if some kind of message was passing between them.

'Get yourself a drink,' she said.

I'd had enough by then. I wasn't going to find out anything useful now, and whatever it was they were up to, I wanted to be out of it. It was time to go.

'I'm off,' I said. 'Thanks for the drink.'

'Oh,' she said, making a disappointed face. 'Well, if you want to ask me anything more, come up and see me sometime. At the office. I'm usually free around lunchtime.'

She gave me a slow smile. I was sure she was vamping me

up, but I couldn't tell whether or not she meant it.

'Okay,' I said, 'I'll see you.'

I nodded to Frank, ignored Parker and walked over to the machine where Aubrey was shooting down alien spacecraft.

'Hang on a bit,' he said, and I waited until the end of the game. Then we went. There was still an inch of orange in his glass and on the way out he took it back to the bar and put it down carefully.

Parker was waiting outside at the end of the driveway. There were three men in donkey jackets with him, all of them large, with the massive thick-necked look of men who swung picks and carried bricks for a living.

'Party time,' I said to Aubrey, and I heard him snickering quietly. As we got closer the men spread out to block our way. Parker was in the centre and he pointed at me.

'I thought I told you,' he said. 'Stay away from my family.'

All of a sudden I was angry.

'Hasn't it occurred to you by now,' I asked him, 'that I don't give a bugger?'

'Black cunt,' he shouted.

That was it. We were going to get it on. I saw his face tighten before he lunged at me and I ducked out of range.

It was at times like these that I blessed the stupidity of my old PE teacher. He'd been certain that a strong black boy like me could make a career for himself as a boxer, and pressured me into the school team before I could work up the courage to resist. It took me a year to work my way out, but in the meantime I'd hated being hit, and I became good at dodging and blocking punches. Parker never laid a glove on me. It was Aubrey's activities which nearly proved my undoing.

When Keith threw the first punch at me Aubrey had launched himself straight at the nearest one of the donkey jackets, and I'd caught a glimpse of him springing on one leg, the other kicking furiously into the air. After that I had been ducking and weaving round Parker and I'd lost sight of the rest of the action.

It was easier than I'd thought it would be, because he was slow and ponderous and every time he tried to hit me I saw it coming. We'd got on to the grass after a little while, and to discourage him I hit him with two hard slaps, right and left, bam bam. He stood still for a moment, and I was just congratulating myself on my cleverness when a heavy body knocked into me, and by the time I recovered my balance Parker had me by the throat. I reached up to grab one of his fingers, but he shifted his grip and got his right arm round my waist with the other up under my chin.

I could smell his horrible beer breath coming at me in suffocating gusts. My rage had gone after the first moment, and I shut the pain and the stink out and concentrated on the solution. I had it almost immediately, and I lifted my leg as if I was trying to knee him and, instead, stomped my foot down hard on his instep. At the same time I twisted my body and brought both arms round to break his hold.

I ended up a few yards away, panting and rubbing my throat where he'd squeezed it. In the circumstances it was a comfort to see him sitting on the grass nursing his foot.

'Oi,' Aubrey called out from the gate. 'You coming?'

I looked around. Two of Parker's companions were lying on the ground, one flat out, the other holding his lower half and groaning. The third man was limping slowly up the steps of the building.

'What are you, Aubrey?' I said. 'Bloody Superman?'

'Nah. Them guys are probably okay if they can hold you and hit you. Beat you up bad. But they all got these big bellies. You notice that? Move around a little bit and they be so tired they fall over.'

We went out to the street and got back into the car. On the way I looked back a couple of times, but no one seemed interested in following us.

Chapter 19

That night I started going through Kim's diary. I'd looked at it before but when I'd discovered that the names were mostly represented by initials, making it a sort of code, I'd put it aside with the intention of tackling it later. I didn't feel now as if it could get much later. I had a suspicion that the longer Borelli spent making a case against Tony, the harder it would be to explode it.

I'd come across a nest of snakes crawling with various motives for doing away with Aston, but viewed from a distance all of it would seem like ordinary office intrigue or the robust give and take of local politics. 'Woman's bloody chatter,' Borelli would say. And in any case I had a suspicion that the cops would be extremely cautious about getting involved in anything that could be interpreted as political. What they had on Tony was obvious and, if you had to explain it to a jury, nice and easy to understand. The irony was that a lot of what I'd found out in the last few days would harden up a case against Tony and Suzanne. A love triangle. A jealous wife. A passionate young lover. I had rejected the obvious conclusions because she was my friend and I loved her, but Borelli wouldn't be all that far behind me, and Suzanne might be in more danger than she thought.

The diary only ran from the beginning of the year and,

slowly, I began to make sense of the references. A stood for Aston, M I took to be her mother – Mum. The monster, fully spelled out every time he was mentioned, had to be her father.

I went back to the beginning once I'd got the basics straight. It had been a long day and I was having difficulty in concentrating. I'd dropped Aubrey off at home, and gone in with him to see Maman. She had a meal ready for us and it was well past midnight before I got away. At that hour I could stay awake easily enough. Making sense of what I read was another matter.

Eventually different strands began to emerge. One strand was about Aston and her feelings about him, another was about her parents and the arguments which raged between them, another was about work and her ambitions.

There was a short list of what I took to be New Year's resolutions on the first page.

>Stop being frightened. Be more open.
>Do more singing. Remember the feeling I got from being in *Saint Nicholas*.
>Do postgraduate. Stop putting it off.
>Support M. None of it her fault.
>Tell Mar to fuck off.
>Be more positive with A. Courage girl.

Underneath all this was the last sentence in capital letters.

A NEW LIFE STARTS HERE

There was something unpleasantly eerie about sitting there at that hour of night, reading the secret thoughts of someone I had never met, and for a moment it felt like crouching in front of a keyhole, peering in.

The next entry said something about the monster not having recovered from the holiday and being drunk, again. She'd broken her first New Year's resolution and left M to it. And so it went on. Some pages were blank. There were a couple of poems I didn't recognise. Aston kept on cropping up in a routine fashion. One or two references were ecstatic. Feb.14 said: 'Champagne, Chopin, and A. Totally blown away.' On a couple of other days she wrote that she couldn't stand it any more. The last entry in the book said merely: 'TEST! the big one.'

After that the book was blank. I flipped back through the pages. Now I had a grasp of the storylines it was easier. All the entries about her parents denoted some kind of row. At one point she wrote: 'Absolutely no saving graces about the monster. I despise him so utterly it's hard to believe he's my father.'

There were other entries about visits from friends, trips out of London, and so on. Another page mentioned Mar, who I took to be Marcie. 'Mar came round. Talked about the TROUBLE. How she's changed. Now she's my dearest relative and best friend. It's all about A, of course. But I have no intention of getting involved. They're bound to lose anyway. A is so much more astute than they imagine. He'll ruin them and I'll just have to learn to cope with that.'

I read this bit with a surge of excitement. I got up and walked around. I had to talk to her, because it was obvious she knew the secret of whatever it was Aston had discovered about the Parker clan. It would provide a solid motive, and at the back of my mind I had Keith Parker lined up as the most likely suspect.

I leafed through the rest of the pages but there were no more hints, so I put it down and lay back to think about it, and in a moment I was asleep.

I woke up with the sun in my eyes and the usual cramps and aches from sleeping corkscrewed into the armchair. But the article was on my mind. It's like that with some of them. I'd fiddle around for ages and then suddenly it would be all I could think about. I sat down to write the first sentence, then tore it out and started again. After a couple of hours of this it began to work and soon I was pounding away in a rhythm that felt unstoppable.

Aston and his background, his days at the factory, what kind of man and politician he'd been, what his friends and enemies said about him, the racial tensions in the party he'd represented; all this flowed smoothly into my head and through to the page.

Halfway through I realised something was missing. I'd

forgotten a name. I got out the notebook where I jotted things down at the end of the day, but it wasn't there. In fact I hadn't made any notes at all about the previous day. Stupid. Stupid.

I rang Marcie's office at the civic centre. When she answered her voice was cool and preoccupied. I made it formal, apologising for disturbing her and asking her to repeat what she'd said about the housing project she'd mentioned.

'Kitchener Avenue?'

'That's right. That's the one.'

'Oh. I didn't think you were very interested.'

'I was interested in everything you said,' I told her. 'But I intended to quote you on this and I wanted to get it right.'

That seemed to warm her up and she began telling me about it with what sounded like enthusiasm. But almost as soon as she'd begun she paused in the middle of a sentence.

'Wait a minute,' she said. 'I've got a meeting near there tonight. Would you like to come and see it?'

I hesitated. I had enough to finish the article I was writing, but seeing her without Frank or Keith present might provide me with a chance to find out something about her problems with Aston. She might even tell me where Kim was, although I doubted that.

'I'd love to come,' I said.

'Good. It's worth seeing.'

She told me where to meet her and the time. While she was doing so the image of her hand crossed my mind. Then I thought about her legs.

'Don't be late,' she said. 'It's not a place where I want to hang about.'

'No chance,' I told her.

Chapter 20

I finished the article about mid-afternoon and, impatient to be done with it and to get it off my hands, I drove over to South London.

The features editor greeted me with a raised eyebrow.

'I was just beginning to worry,' she said.

They're all the same, editors, men and women, and I swear that if they ever appointed an eleven-year-old girl child to the job, it would only take her a couple of days to acquire the cool stare and the distant tone. This one was actually younger than me, with the bright pink cheeks, yellow hair and china-blue eyes of a doll. But behind her desk, encased in her grey pinstriped suit, it was impossible to think of her as anything but a figure of authority.

I pulled up a chair and sat on the other side of her desk while she skimmed through the pages. At the end she looked up and, because she was one of the nicer specimens of the breed, she gave me a small tight smile.

'Problems?'

She shook her head.

'No. Seems okay on first reading. If there's anything later on I'll give you a ring. We'll probably run it day after tomorrow, with a little piece about the inquest.'

I nodded sagely. I hadn't known about the time of the inquest, or remembered it at all, but it wouldn't do to let on.

I was home in less than an hour. As usual, after finishing the work, I was keyed up. The tension had gone but I was still riding high on adrenalin, full of confidence and the conviction that I could sort out problems, unravel puzzles, make things happen. I rang Sophie.

'Hello stranger,' I said. 'What about tonight?'

She sounded genuinely regretful.

'I can't. I fixed up to see this woman.'

'Spid?'

'Yes. I rang her today and she was really nice. She remembered me and she's quite happy to do some more.'

I found it hard to think of Spid as nice, but maybe what I'd seen of her was out of character, or perhaps it was to do with being a man.

I bit back my first reaction. I could hardly complain, but I didn't expect anything to come out of Sophie's efforts. On the other hand, there had been an undertone of excitement when she'd first mentioned the project which made me wary of pouring cold water on it.

It wasn't simply, I thought, the prospect of sharing something in which I was wrapped up, coming in from the cold. There was also the secret delight of joining the process of detection and investigation. The thrill of the chase. And on top of all that were her professional instincts. Many photographers were incurious about the reporter's trade. Others thought that some of the reporters they worked with were wallies, and knew they could do much better. Sophie was one of them, and she was driven by a restless ambition which would make her seize any opportunity to master a new skill.

'How are you going to work it?' I asked. I was curious now.

'I don't know. Flatter her a bit. You know. Bring the subject up casually. See what she says. It's bound to be on her mind. Maybe she'll say something helpful. I mean I'm not going to ask her straight out, where's Kim?'

'Well, remember she's insanely suspicious.'

'Don't worry,' she said. 'When you spend time taking pictures with people it's very intimate. Sometimes they tell you personal things that they won't tell anyone else.'

She was probably right.

'I suppose you're right,' I told her. 'But take it easy. Just listen for anything which may be useful, about Aston, or about any crafty fiddles that have been going on.'

'*Sí señor,*' she said.

'And be careful, *mujer*. She's got some rough friends.'

She laughed.

'Don't worry. I won't see those women, and if I do, I'll send for you.'

The conversation hadn't been totally reassuring, but I was still on the ball, buoyed up by the euphoria of getting through the article.

I rang Suzie. She said she had to hurry because she had an appointment with their accountant. I said I'd only rung to see how she was and how were things. She said things were as well as could be expected, Helen said hello, and was there anything special. I said good, good and no.

'By the way.' Abruptly. 'Shelagh Parker rang me. I asked her round tomorrow afternoon, after that business.'

I took it she meant the inquest.

'You'll be there?'

'Yes. Of course.'

'You can come back with us afterwards.'

A businesslike flourish on which to end. But when I hung up I wondered how well she really was, and what was going on between the two women there in the house of the dead.

The phone rang again. It was Sophie, her voice quick and excited.

'Look in the evening paper. There's a piece about Aston. Well, not really about Aston. The housing estate, but it mentions Aston. Look on page two.'

I hadn't bought the evening paper.

'Tell me what it says.'

'No time. Ring me tomorrow. Bye.'

I went downstairs and got the evening paper. There was the

usual picture of Aston, decorated with the headline 'Police Raid Death Estate'.

Below was a short piece which said that following the death of Councillor Edwards, controversial chair of construction services in the North London borough, police had visited the youth project near which his body had been found and taken away documents. The centre had been dogged by scandal and rumour even before being opened recently by Councillor Edwards. Spokesmen for the local council and the police had made a statement to the effect that they were investigating charges of embezzlement.

The connection was a natural one for a newspaper to make. At the same time I had a feeling that someone else was trying to narrow the angle, and if I had to place a bet, I'd have put my money on Kevin Sparks, master of the press handout.

I rang Aubrey and told him I'd be round later. I had an idea, but I didn't want to tell him about it just yet.

He said he'd wait.

In the street the traffic was beginning to thin out. Chummy's Porsche rolled up, and he parked it carefully on the opposite side of the street. Then he got out and walked around it a couple of times, looking at the paintwork and the bumpers. The girl with him, a lithe blonde with ringlets that brushed her shoulders, power dressed in black silk and high heels, crossed the road slowly, waiting till he stopped circling the car and scooted over. His round jowly face was split by a grin, and he paid no attention that I could see to the traffic.

In a moment I heard the door slam and their footsteps mounting the stairs. Then, almost immediately, the first notes of a Spanish guitar. Chummy had all the latest CD equipment and killer speakers. Ace. The reproduction was literally amazing and he could make it sound as if every last one of the Gypsy Kings were raving their heads off downstairs.

In some moods I liked the noise of the music, at other times I could have gone down and pitched the lot out of his window. But in the centre of London the size and flimsiness of modern flats breeds a different kind of awareness. In the last twenty years I'd grown accustomed to the noise of my neighbours arguing, playing music, and bonking. By now it was probably as natural to me as the sound of the sea would be to a sailor.

If things went according to pattern the music would go off in about an hour and the couple would emerge and walk to the brasserie on the corner. Sometimes an Indian waiter in a white jacket would deliver a meal, complete with a rose carefully balanced on the top of the white plastic bag. In that case the music would go off in about another hour, to be replaced by more human sounds. Like the tide and the seasons it was a cycle, awesome in its repetitiveness and inevitability.

I left Chummy to it and drove down to Paddington to pick up Aubrey. Maman was out visiting and we sat round the dining table while I explained what I wanted him to do.

I told him about the article and my idea that various people with vested interests would try and heap suspicion of Aston's killing on the youths around the project. Whether or not Tony was tried it might be a good way of diverting suspicion, as well as clouding Aston's memory. The problem was that I had no way of confirming my sense that no one there had anything to do with it. If I could be sure, I'd go all out to try and pin down whatever it was the town hall crowd were covering up.

'The thing is,' I said, 'that the youths down there won't talk to me.'

Aubrey grinned quickly as if that idea was irrepressibly funny, and I might have been irritated if it had been anyone else.

'I don't think you'll have that problem,' I said. 'If anyone around there did something, there'll be a buzz among the youths even if they're not talking openly. Some people might have disappeared. That kind of thing. That's all I need to know.'

Aubrey didn't answer immediately. He was frowning and it was clear that something about the proposal was causing him trouble. I knew him too well to try and persuade him. If he didn't want to do it, he wouldn't.

'I'll make a deal with you,' he said eventually. 'I'll go down and if the running's cool I'll tell you. If somebody there did anything, is not my business.'

Aubrey's loyalties were different from mine and that was the best I'd get.

'Okay,' I said, 'but be careful. Them guys heavy.'

'Yeah. I know. I know them.'

I stared.

'You know them? How come?'

Aubrey smiled.

'I was away with some of them. We play football sometimes.'

'Why didn't you tell me?'

He shrugged.

'You never asked.'

Later on I drove Aubrey up to North London, and dropped him off near the estate. He was going to work out with the weights at the centre and talk to his friends. For a moment I envied him his calm and clarity of purpose. In comparison I felt scattered and without focus.

The streets around me reflected my mood. It was about nine, a dull cloudy evening, not yet night, but with darkness lurking slyly round every corner.

This was the part of the borough which had, early in the century, come closest to an industrial park, and it was marked out in regular lines by ruler-straight streets, bordered by mean barrack-like houses which should have been pulled down long ago. On the other hand, the fact that they hadn't been replaced during the postwar building booms by giant high rise estates proved eventually to be an unexpected boon.

Kitchener Avenue was a long flat crescent backing on to a disused railway line. The high wire fence around it was decorated with a notice which said that the council – 'working for a better life' – was converting the site into four hundred new homes. Below that it said that the site was guarded by dogs. Work seemed to have stopped for the day although there were still bulldozers and lorries standing about. I got out of the car and went up to the gate, which was standing open. In the distance I could hear sounds of activity, but I hesitated. At that moment I'd remembered that Parker's men would be working on this site, and I wondered also what time the guard dogs came on duty.

'Hello,' I shouted, and in answer Marcie came out from behind a lorry and waved.

'Come on,' she called.

This time she was wearing open flat-heeled shoes and a sleeveless dress with buttons all the way down the front. There was a flat bag slung across her shoulder and her left hand was hidden under the jacket she was carrying.

'I'm not really supposed to be here,' she said. 'But it's a good idea to come down sometimes and see how the work is going. There's always some prat asking for a progress report.'

'Oh. Is it all right to be here?' I asked her. 'I mean, Parker's not going to come round the corner in a minute leading a guard dog, is he? I don't fancy being trapped by that maniac.'

She laughed.

'No. He's not around today. Anyway I imagine he'd be more worried about meeting you. What did you do to him yesterday? He came back into the club limping, and he wouldn't tell us. Frank's theory was that you and that friend of yours set on him and beat him up.'

She looked over her shoulder at me when I didn't answer. She smiled and the green eyes searched for mine.

'Is that right? Is that what you did?'

The thought seemed to excite her.

'Let's just say I made him an offer he didn't refuse.'

She laughed at this, throwing back her head and opening her mouth wide, like someone on a holiday outing. In the next moment she stumbled on the uneven surface and when I put my hand out to help her, she took it and tucked her right hand under my arm, leaning on me a little. From time to time I could feel the softness of her breast as she moved against me.

Walking along like this, she told me more about the project. There was going to be a hypermarket nearby, a few new businesses had taken advantage of various concessions to set up in the neighbourhood, there would be craft workshops and arcades in a couple of old warehouses across the railway line, and the big one – they'd hired Peat Marwick to explore setting up a theme park in partnership with British Rail.

'This is our docklands,' she said. 'But we're going to make it work for our people. They come first. That's what good local government's about.'

Many of these were Aston's ideas, she told me, and once they'd learned the trick of pulling them in, working with private investors hadn't been as difficult as many of the Labour group had feared. Aston's feel for public relations and his credibility with the Left had been invaluable.

The houses were being reclad in new brick. The façades would be kept, but inside they were being reconverted, windows enlarged, rooms added, and modern utilities installed. The architects were brilliant. When it was ready, they were asking Prince Charles himself to declare it open. During this recital she pulled me towards one of the houses on the end of a row. This one would be a show house and it was nearly complete, except for the gas and electricity. It would give me an idea of what they were going to be like.

It was nearly dark now, the evening light a last fitful gleam on the horizon. Inside the house it was dark, the shadows pressing in, just possible to see. The downstairs consisted of a kitchen/diner and a large sitting room looking out on to a tiny garden at the back. It seemed pleasant enough, with light cream-painted walls and some kind of synthetic tiling on the floor. A deal nicer than my leaky old rooms in the attic near Marble Arch.

'There's a couple of bedrooms upstairs,' she said. 'We'll see better up there.'

She sounded subdued now, as if she was reluctant to disturb the silent dusk with too much vivacity. The sound of building work had stopped completely now and I hoped the men hadn't gone out and locked the gate. Going up the stairs the backs of her legs seemed to gather the light and gleam in the shadows.

There were two rooms upstairs, in addition to a bathroom and an airing cupboard. The light grey bathroom suite hadn't been connected yet, and for some reason there were three toilet bowls standing there. I said how nice it was going to look.

Through the back window we could see the railway line clearly in the pale grey light. It was overgrown with wild shrubs and flowers, but it had a pretty, delicately rural look about it. I could picture it as the subject of a water colour.

She unslung her bag and put it down, then slid open the window, using both hands and without bothering to conceal the left one. The single finger pointed aimlessly.

I'd been thinking about opening the window myself, because the house seemed suddenly airless and oppressive, and it was hard to breathe.

Her voice was quieter and deeper now, and, like a conspirator, I had to lean closer to hear it.

'The nuclear train used to come past here. Two in the morning.'

I had seen it, an eerie monster, flashing livid red and yellow lights, puffing and bellowing on its secret way.

I grunted, and she turned, smiling, to look at me. I turned my head at the same time and our lips met.

I hadn't intended it, but once the kiss started, it was violent and implacable. Our mouths mashed together and her tongue stabbed and licked around mine. She gave a faint groan in her throat and we reeled back against the wall next to the window. Our hips moved hard against each other's and I fumbled for a moment and undid her top two buttons, reached into her bra and gripped one of her breasts. She moved back a little and unfastened her belt and the rest of the buttons. Then she reached back, did something and the bra fell away. I put my hand down in front of her, pulled her pants down and stroked the wet parting. She said aah loudly into my mouth, unzipped me with a rapid movement, took out my penis and squeezed it fiercely.

'Wait a moment,' she whispered. 'Wait.'

She bent over, rummaged in her bag, straightened up and handed me a condom. I tore the foil open to put it on, and while I was doing this she slipped the pants all the way off.

'Come,' she said.

She pulled me sideways to where a short plank, a piece of

builder's rubbish I hadn't noticed in the gloom, was standing against the wall. She kicked it over and stood on it, bringing her eyes a little higher than mine, and for an instant she gave me that intense green stare, before they closed and our mouths sank together again.

It was night before we were finished. She seemed to make a lot of noise, groaning and yelping, and for a while part of me was listening anxiously for footsteps on the stair. Then I stopped and I couldn't hear anything except the noises we made moaning and gasping for breath, and the blood roaring in my ears. She was like a rolling, thrusting bundle of energy and we came to the point a few times, but then she would stop and make me stand still, tight packed, tight pressed and locked together, trembling with the tension of it.

Afterwards, she stood with her arms still round my neck, her head resting on my shoulder, till I slipped, deflated, out of her. Then she moved away abruptly, turned her back to me, fastened her dress, picked up the pants and put them in her bag.

'Shall we go?' she said in a matter-of-fact tone, smoothing a hand over her hair.

We went downstairs in silence. The excitement faded slowly, leaving a slack exhausted feeling behind it, and I trembled a little as I negotiated the darkened stairs. Outside the house she put her arm through mine as she had before, leaned on me, and we walked in silence to the gate which was still open. She had a smug, amused expression on her face, and from time to time she looked round and smiled at me.

I smiled back, but I could feel myself beginning to worry. If everything I'd heard about Marcie was true, this could have been a whopper of a mistake.

We went through the gate and she pulled it shut behind her. She looked at her watch. I couldn't quite make it out, but the time looked to be well past ten.

'Security should be here soon,' she said.

I nodded, hovering, a little uncertain about what to do next. I wanted to get away and think.

She took a fast step, put one arm round my neck and kissed

me, pressing her body hard against mine.

'That was nice,' she whispered in my ear. 'We must do it again. Soon.'

'Okay,' I whispered back, and she let go and stepped away from me.

'Ring me,' she said in her normal voice, and then turned, walked away and got into a new white Golf parked almost opposite my old banger. I got into mine and pulled out behind her, following the cherry-red tail lights until they turned into the main road out of the district and I lost them in the stream of traffic.

Chapter 21

The coroner had thinning sandy hair, gold-rimmed specs and an air of mild benevolence which could turn stern and angry in a flash. I had the sense that all the way through his evidence Borelli was watching him warily, just in case he started something.

The inquest was in the old court building, and there was a gruesome congruity about the fact that the last time we'd been there had been for Tony's remand. I recognised a lot of the faces there. The press officer of Aston's union, a man I'd worked with years ago, gave me a sad little wave. Eva and Margaret had turned up and were sitting stiffly at the back. Spid, Vijay and Walter were all there, sitting in separate parts of the room. I nodded at Walter and he nodded back with a sort of speculative stare.

Keith Parker wasn't present but Kevin Sparks was sitting next to Shelagh Parker, her face masked by the dark glasses. Marcie was on the other side of her. A memory of the previous night flashed through my mind and there was a little surge of excitement somewhere inside me. I hadn't been sure I wanted to see her, but I think I had been hoping that I would.

I still wasn't clear what I felt about the event. I'd gone straight home and mooched around aimlessly for a while. Then I'd gone to bed and dreamt about pursuing Sophie through a long series of empty rooms, never catching her, but always on the verge of an agonising orgasm.

In the morning I felt both apprehensive and exhilarated. What had happened must have made me vulnerable and I had no way of telling how Marcie might use it. On the other hand I was certain that it was the most thrilling thing that had happened to me for a long time.

Before setting out I'd rung Aubrey to ask how he'd made out at the youth centre.

'Nothing going on,' he'd said immediately. 'Maybe a little crack, but they don't know anything about what happened to Aston.'

'Okay.'

I could take Aubrey's word for it, I thought. He was part of the scene, and his antennae would tell him what was going on.

'I'll go up one more time tonight. But I reckon you can forget about it.'

'Okay.'

'One thing more. Police plentiful round there. They came the other day, took some papers. Then they search the place. Now they asking questions. About Tony. If Tony came there often. Who he was friends with. If he was with Dalton. See they interested in Dalton.'

'Dalton?'

'Yes. Asking questions about him. If he talk to Tony. Anybody see him with Aston. If he give out any drugs. Them youths think they working up to plant him. Could be trouble.'

I had thought about it. I didn't know what to make of all that except that Borelli was going round the bend or trying to stir something up. Later on, giving his evidence, he had a smoothly truculent air, like a football manager, honest Joe under pressure.

The proceedings went quickly. I had the impression that the coroner wanted the whole thing over with as fast as possible. There were diagrams of the estate, the street where Aston had been found. A doctor talked about the wound. He had died instantly. The whole affair didn't seem to be very much to do with Aston.

Towards the end of the morning the coroner spoke about his sympathy for Suzanne, looking directly at her and Helen, sitting at the front. She looked back at him and nodded soberly as if they were talking together in private, and it struck me that he might well have been somebody they'd had dinner with. A friend.

Then it was over. In the lobby afterwards Suzie and Helen came past, hurrying to avoid the reporters. Suzie just paused a second to speak to me in a low voice.

'In a shortish while,' she said. 'See you.'

On the pavement outside I hurried to catch up with Eva and Margaret. Margaret gave me a cautious hello.

'How's Tony?'

Eva stopped and faced me.

'Not too good. We were hoping they would drop the case, but they seem to be going ahead.'

Resilient. She didn't look crushed by the thought.

'It looks not too bad, though,' she said. 'People saw him. We've got some witnesses. And the lawyer says their case isn't strong. We just have to hope and trust in God.'

I told her I thought there might be developments in other directions. Her lawyer, I said, ought to get in touch with Tommy, who could be a character witness. He was a sharp old man, I said, who would not be intimidated by the court and could probably impress a jury.

'Tommy,' she said. 'That old rascal. I'd forgotten about him.'

So had I. I looked around. He hadn't turned up but it didn't mean anything. The thought of coming might have upset him.

When the two women had gone I looked around for Borelli, but he had disappeared; so had the Parkers and all the town hall people. There was no point in hanging around. I got the car out and drove up to Suzie's.

On the way I thought about what I had told Eva. The problem was that if Aubrey had it right Borelli was looking in very different directions and, for someone like him, I could see the logic of trying to link Aston, Tony, Dalton and the problem of drugs on the estate. It was a case where simple answers guaranteed devious and complicated results.

If the police continued their present line, there could well be a small riot at the centre, and that would muddy the waters even further. In that event things wouldn't look very good for Tony. But there seemed to be very little I could do. It would be a waste of time approaching Borelli. He wouldn't listen to me unless I had hard evidence and all I had was suspicion and a lot of gossip. I wasn't even sure, any more, what I was doing.

Tommy opened the door at Suzie's house. He was wearing a black suit, and he looked smaller, as if he'd shrunk overnight.

'I heard you were coming,' he said as if he'd caught me out. Then he turned and led the way into the big sitting room.

There were half a dozen bottles of rum on the coffee table, one of them open. So that's where it comes from, I thought. But then it occurred to me that perhaps it was the other way round and now that Aston was gone Suzie was restoring them to Tommy.

She was sitting on the sofa next to Shelagh, and there were coffee things, cups and a jug, in front of them. But while Suzie was sipping from her cup, Shelagh had a glass of rum in her hand and, as I came in the door, she drained it quickly.

Tommy sat down and poured another tot for the two of them, then one for me, as an afterthought. He looked at home, as he always did in female company. He had a suitably mournful air, but underneath it there was a powerful current of energy and delight. That's how he was, and I didn't blame him. Both the women were beautiful, and together they presented a contrast which commanded the attention.

Suzanne was taller, and this morning she had a drawn fine-boned look, accentuated by the way her hair was pulled back from her face. She'd plaited it into a long tail with a black ribbon threaded through it, and the style made her look stately and girlish at the same time.

Shelagh's hair was wavy with a bronzish tint and, unlike Suzie, who went pink easily and was inclined to freckles, her skin had a creamy opaque undertone.

We shook hands. She was in black too and still wearing dark

glasses but she didn't seem as nervous as she had been when we met before. Instead she gave me an enigmatic smile, and I wondered whether Marcie had said anything about me to her. But that was probably paranoia, I thought.

'Where's Helen?' I asked.

'Upstairs, packing,' Suzie said. 'We're going home in a little while. I'm going to drive her down.'

'Get away from here,' Tommy said. 'That's the best thing.'

He shook his head as if he'd invented the idea.

'How's Miss Argentina?' Suzie asked me.

There was something happening between her and Shelagh when she said this. Not so much as a look, more of a vibe that I felt. Both of them looked at me. Tommy sniggered.

Suzanne had met Sophie who, on that occasion, had been a little sullen and withdrawn. Not appealing. Afterwards she told me that she'd found Suzanne's manner 'like a queen bee', irritatingly proprietorial. Suzie, in her turn, told me that this wasn't the woman for me, and after that always referred to her as Miss Argentina. I had the suspicion that, although Suzie often denounced English narrowness and xenophobia, she was annoyed by Sophie's foreign manners and accent.

'Miss Argentina's fine,' I said. 'And her name's Sophie, as you well know.'

She smiled and shrugged.

'Sorry.' She set her cup down firmly. 'Tommy,' she said. 'Let's go sort out that stuff you want before I go.'

I wondered what Tommy was after, and I wondered also what she would do with the rest of Aston's belongings. I made a mental note to ask her sometime.

They went out of the room with her hand at his elbow. She had a concerned air, as if Tommy was the chief mourner. I looked back at Shelagh, and she was gazing straight at me, safe behind the dark glasses.

'I must go myself,' she murmured.

She had a light soft voice, without the hard edges of Suzanne or Marcie's.

'Look,' I said. 'I'm sorry if I hassled you the other day. I didn't mean to. Your husband seemed very upset.'

She shook her head, a rapid, almost convulsive gesture.

'I wasn't bothered. It's just that I didn't know who you were and we've had bad experiences with the press. You know.'

'Of course,' I said.

Her glass was empty and I leaned over and poured more rum into it. She picked it up immediately and took a swallow.

'Anyway,' she said. 'I don't know anything about all that business.'

She sounded more animated, but she seemed to have forgotten that I was asking about Kim.

'Doesn't matter,' I said. 'What you don't realise is that I'm a fan of yours.'

She frowned.

'What?'

'I saw some of your paintings at the central library. Oh, ages ago. I really liked them.'

That got her. She put one hand to the glasses as if she wanted to see me more clearly.

'You didn't,' she said. 'You couldn't have remembered.'

She sounded pleased and excited. Any kind of artist is a sucker for the flattery of attention, especially if circumstances force privacy on their efforts. Actually, when I sensed her delight I felt a bit guilty about the lies I was going to tell, but the actor in me loved it. Manipulating bastard, Suzie used to say when she was angry with me.

'I remember very well,' I said. 'On the opening night someone pointed you out to me. I think it was you, and I wanted to talk to you then about the pictures, but you looked busy, and I left it.'

'Yes,' she said reflectively. 'I suppose I was.'

'The thing is,' I said, 'I don't know much about art but I thought they had an extremely sensitive feel for the place.'

I could see her blushing.

'Thank you.'

I told her how I'd grown up in the district, and I had thought she must have as well.

'I did,' she said.

She'd lived off the High Street, not far from the old town hall. I asked her if she remembered the old alleyway beside the cemetery, and when she said she did, I told her how I used to go there with my girlfriend and do naughty things.

I watched her closely for cues. She was smiling, then she looked serious.

'I wish I'd done things like that when I was that age,' she said. 'But we had a strict Catholic upbringing. In by ten. No boys.'

I laughed sympathetically. Just then Helen came into the room and stopped, looking round as if she'd forgotten something. Then she went over to the table and picked up a couple of books and a writing pad she'd left there. She went back to the door and paused again.

'Sammy,' she said. 'I'm taking Suzanne back with me. Do you have my number?'

I told her it was in my old address book, and she went out, closing the door behind her. She hadn't sounded very chummy and I supposed that she had been upset by the inquest. In any case our chattering wasn't very appropriate in the circumstances.

Shelagh must have had the same thought, because she picked up her handbag.

'I must go,' she said.

'Have you got your car?' I asked her.

I was going to recommend against her driving anywhere. She'd put down half the bottle while we sat there, and she didn't show any real signs of unsteadiness, but in her place I'd have been pissed legless. She was either a serious tippler, or she was underestimating the strength of the stuff. Maybe both, because her face was flushed and her voice was louder than it had been.

She shook her head with that convulsive motion.

'I don't drive.'

'I'll take you back.'

'No.'

'Don't worry,' I said. 'I'll drop you a couple of streets away. No one will see me.'

'Okay.'

We said goodbye. Suzanne put her arms round my neck and hugged me tight. Then she relaxed a little and whispered: 'Is it all right?'

'I'll let you know,' I told her in a low voice. 'I'll ring you.'

Outside the house Shelagh teetered a little on her high heels, but she didn't burst into song or anything extreme.

'It sounds terrible,' she said. 'But all that really depressed me. I couldn't refuse to go, but I don't think I could have got through it completely sober.'

'No. I know what you mean.'

I did. But I suspected also that she didn't entirely reciprocate Suzanne's liking for her. Suzie had the kind of self-confidence which often stopped her perceiving other people's coldness or dislike.

'Can you stop here,' Shelagh said. 'I think I'll take a walk. I don't want to go home yet.'

'I'll be frank with you, me old china,' I said. 'If you go walking around out there you'll probably sit down on the nearest park bench and go to sleep and you wouldn't want that. Let's go have a coffee, talk some more, then you go home in a taxi.'

She considered this, a little owlish in the dark glasses. She screwed up her mouth, pouting. When she did that it blossomed into a red flower.

'Not around here,' she said.

'No. We'll go to my place.' And before she could say anything, I hurried on. 'You'll be certain of not being seen there.'

'Okay.'

We scooted up to the centre of town in silence. I couldn't tell what she was thinking, but I kept looking into my rear view mirror. Somehow the fantasy of Parker suddenly looming up behind us kept running through my mind.

Nothing happened and I drew up in front of my door with relief. My lucky day. There was even a parking space.

We hurried across the pavement. She seemed sober now, but her nerves had come back, because she tied a scarf round her head, and kept looking round as we went in the door.

Upstairs I told her I was going to have a drink to settle my nerves, and she said she'd like one as well. I meant it too. Coming up behind her I had remembered climbing the stairs at Kitchener Avenue with Marcie. It seemed a long time ago.

I sat next to her on the sofa. She smiled and raised her eyebrows interrogatively when she saw me looking.

'What?'

'The glasses. Makes me nervous. You look at me and I can't see your eyes.'

She looked seriously at me for a couple of seconds, then she reached up and took them off. She had warm, smokey-blue eyes, with a dark red bruise, tinged with blue, under one of them. She stared steadily at me.

'Someone been hitting you?'

She looked away from me quickly, hiding the eye, then she looked straight back.

'Why did you bring me here?'

My turn not to answer. Instead, I reached out and stroked her cheek, then when she didn't move or look away, I put my hand behind her neck and drew us closer, till we came together in the middle of the sofa. She held her lips up to me and I kissed her. Her body felt warm and relaxed, nothing nervous about her. I stroked her breasts gently and she pressed her lips repeatedly to my face. In a little while I got up and pulled her to her feet and we went next door and got into bed.

Chapter 22

In the end I simply asked her.

She was lying next to me, propped up on one elbow, her hair shading out one side of her face. Close up I could see that her mouth was wider and her lips fuller than I'd realised, because her broad cheekbones made them seem smaller. I stroked her breasts, which were also bigger than I'd imagined, and touching them made me want to start again.

'There was this girl down the road who went to St Paul's. She was so confident, always going out. The life and soul, and I had this fantasy about going there as well. Funny really. Frank, my brother, used to laugh at me. That's a devil of a thing for a nice Catholic girl he'd say. A devil of a thing.'

She laughed.

'He used to take them off after he came back from holidays in Ireland. What's that you're up to now, he used to say, I don't trust you biddies over the water. At all. At all.'

She giggled, remembering.

'He wanted to go and live there. Then he went to work for Parker's. Poor Frank.'

'What was wrong with that?'

She was silent for a moment, thinking it over.

'I don't know. Something about the Parkers. The way they were. He was really very sensitive, you know, and it destroyed something about him. He used to laugh at the old man, then suddenly he agreed with everything he said.'

She stopped and looked away from me.

'Drink. The curse of the Connors.' She laughed and looked back at me. 'I can talk. A nice Catholic girl.'

She shook her head reflectively, her mood changing again.

'I wanted Kim to go to St Paul's. Be different, I suppose. But she ended up with the nuns, same as I did.'

I'd heard that before. So many of the women I'd met had wanted to be one of those girls, commanding and accomplished.

'Is that what Keith wanted?' I asked.

'I don't want to talk about him,' she said abruptly. She lay flat, trapping my hand under her, her chin on the pillow, staring straight at the wall.

'That bad, huh?'

She turned her face to me. We looked into each other's eyes.

'What time is it?' she whispered. 'I've got to go soon.'

'When do you have to get back home?'

'I don't know. Depends on where I've been.'

'Not yet.'

She tilted her lips to mine and brought her body full up against me. I put my arms round her and we started again.

Afterwards, without my noticing it, the thin column of sunlight through the gap in the window had travelled across the floor at the foot of the bed and begun slanting up the wall. Outside the window I could hear the pigeons cooing.

Shelagh came back from the bathroom, with her face made up and the rest of her neatly tucked into her underwear, the black material dramatic against her creamy flesh. She picked up her dress and worked it up round her.

'Shelagh,' I said. 'I have to talk to Kim. Can you tell me where she is?'

She zipped herself up then sat on the bed to buckle the straps on her shoes.

'Why is talking to Kim so important? What's all this to do with her?'

'Aston was involved in a number of things. She did his research. She was around with him. They were close. She's bound to know something.'

She'd finished with the shoes, but she stayed sitting on the side of the bed, her head bowed, her legs stretched out, elbows on her thighs, hands together between her knees. Her hair had swung over her shoulder in front of her, and I could see the colour staining the back of her neck.

'She doesn't know anything, she doesn't want to be involved. That's why she's gone away.'

'Didn't the police talk to her?'

Her voice sounded shrill and indignant.

'No. Why should they? She only worked there, and she hadn't been doing very much lately anyway.'

The note in her voice was as false as a cracked bell, and something she'd said before flashed through my mind — I don't know anything about all that business.

Maybe, I thought, she dealt with the problems of her life like a Mafia wife, making sure that she didn't know, refusing all responsibility.

'Don't know. Don't care,' I said.

She picked up the feeling in my voice, because she reached out for her bag immediately.

'I must go.'

Suddenly the conversation seemed grotesque. Perhaps it was the hypocrisy I'd practised on her which made me unable to endure the pretence in which I felt she was engaged. I put my hand on her arm and she came back to her previous position, facing stiffly away from me.

'Listen to me, Shelagh,' I said. 'I can't stand this dancing around each other. Not after this afternoon. I'm not out to hurt you or Kim. Anyway, I really like you. Now I know you, just looking at your eye makes me want to get my hands on Keith again and smash his face in. I know that wouldn't help but the point is that I'm on your side. You don't have to bullshit me like this. I know you know that Kim and Aston were more than just distant colleagues.'

She stirred but it was simply to change position. She raised her hands and rested her face in them, holding her cheeks between the open palms.

'But you've got to understand this,' I went on. 'To me Aston wasn't just a black man with political ambitions. He was a kid I played cricket with in our street, and we went swimming and we made kites together. Big monsters. We stuck a razor blade in the tail to cut the strings on other kites, and one time we had a fight, him and me, and I made his nose bleed. The blood never came out my shirt, and I could only wear it at home.'

I was carried away now and hurrying because it felt as if I was explaining something to myself and I couldn't stop.

'I don't know what you thought about him, or whether you approved or whether you thought he'd ruined your daughter, and I don't care. I really don't. The thing is I can't believe that if Kim cared about him she'd want to walk away and say she wasn't involved. I don't blame you for protecting your child. I'd want to do the same for mine, but I'm not after her. I don't want to hurt her and I don't believe that she has anything to say that would hurt you or your family. No more than you're hurting now anyway. Just let her make the choice. Get her to make contact with me or let me know where she is because I need to talk to her. That's all.'

'I don't know where she is,' she said immediately. She took a quick look round at me. She was frowning, her eyes narrow slits under the drawn-down brows. 'I'm not just saying that. I really don't know.'

'Come on. You or Keith must know where to contact her.'

'You don't understand,' she said. 'But she wouldn't tell him anyway. She didn't speak to me either before she left.'

I remembered the nuns.

'Jeez,' I said. 'Is that what you lot do? Never darken my door again.'

She sounded angry, her voice rising into shrillness again, with a slightly wailing tearful undertone.

'You don't understand. She didn't want to talk to me. I tried but she wouldn't.'

'Why? Did you have a go at her? About Aston?'

She shook her head, a movement just barely perceptible. Her hair was hanging round her face, and in the reflected glow of the afternoon sun she was masked now, behind a curtain of shining gold. In the silence of the room I heard a rush of wings from outside the window. A couple of car horns sounded. Sudden angry hoots, and I could imagine the long lines of traffic downstairs in the street. It was getting late.

'Marcie told her,' she said. The curtain rippled. 'It was a long time ago, and only once. In the afternoon. Like now. But Marcie saw us, or someone who did told her. She guessed. She said it was time I had some fun. I'd forgotten about it. It was years since I'd seen Aston except to say hello, then last week Kim rang and left a message on the machine. She said she didn't want to see me and she was going away to think about things. I rang Marcie and she said that Kim had got it out of her. But I don't believe that.'

She reached down into her bag, took a handful of tissues and, still turned away from me, blew her nose and wiped her eyes carefully.

Marcie had struck again, and when that thought crossed my mind it also occurred to me that I was in big trouble.

'Keith heard the message.'

She gave a little laugh.

'I used to think that was the worst thing that could happen. But it was a sort of relief when it came to it. It was difficult. The worst of it was Frank. He knew. I don't know how. Marcie, I suppose, and he came round and kept telling Keith to do something about it. I overheard him. Your dad would have pissed on them, he kept saying. If I had the guts I'd have thrown him out of the house. My own brother.' She shook her head. 'Somehow Frank expected Keith to take old Parker's place, and it was as if he was disappointed that he wasn't exactly the same, couldn't do the same things. I think Keith would have been different if Frank hadn't always been on at him about who he was, about what his dad would have done. All that.'

She paused. She put her right hand round the back of her neck and held it like that. Her voice was muffled now.

'I don't know where Kim is, what she's feeling or thinking. I don't know what she's going to do. I just don't know.'

More than I'd bargained for by a long way. Her bag had tipped over on its side when she'd fumbled with it before, and she began shovelling things back into it.

'Perhaps I can do something about it,' I said. 'If I can see her I can tell her to get in contact with you. I can tell her how you feel.'

'I can't help,' she said. 'I'm useless. I don't know where to begin.'

'Isn't there a friend or someone she'd go to? Someone she trusts?'

'I've thought of that,' she said. 'There's a girl she met at university. She came to stay with us. But I don't know where she lives. She worked for the social services in Bristol. I rang there and they said she'd left the city. I don't know where she's gone. She could even be abroad.'

'What's her name?'

'Sara. Sara. I can't remember the rest of it. It was on the tip of my tongue. I know it.' Panic. She straightened and swung round to gaze at me, eyes wide.

'Take a moment. Think.'

'Sara Castle.'

Almost in the same moment I leapt up and ran for the next room. As I sprang past her, she shrank away towards the corner of the bed, against the wall. I took no notice, because in my head I was busy berating myself for being a perishing idiot.

It's a sin and a shame the way the blind spots creep up and get you. Maybe Freud could have told me why, maybe it was the way that memory works as you get older, but I'd forgotten about the letter. I had glanced at it, thought I'd look at it again some other time, tucked into the cover of the diary, and shoved the lot into my desk. The moment that Shelagh said the name, though, I'd begun to remember the signature at the bottom of the sheet of paper, big flourishing letters, starting with an S.

I opened the desk, picked up the diary and took out the letter. It was signed Sara right enough but there was no address at the top right hand corner. All it said was 'Republic of Handsworth'.

I thought for a moment. I had hoped for an address, but a general location was the next best thing. I put the diary back in the drawer and went back to the bedroom.

Shelagh was standing in front of the mirror, handbag under her arm, dabbing at her face, and she turned to look at me as I came in the door.

'I think we're in business,' I told her.

Chapter 23

The great religions of the world convinced me about it long ago, and if there was any doubt in my mind, environmental science and the new physics turned up to nail the coffin shut.

One day chaos will erupt, the seething waters will begin to rise remorselessly, time will go backwards, the burning sun will turn the earth into empty desert, and famine, pestilence and death will stalk the land.

On that day it will all begin in Handsworth, with packs of dogs, mad with hunger and disease, turning on their human neighbours. They'll begin by attacking the little Asian kids playing out on the pavement and move on to the old white people creeping along, too slow to escape. Then they'll swarm over the Asian shopkeepers, Jamaican patty joint owners, the white TV rental salesmen and the sullen queue outside the social security. They'll devour the council workmen digging up the road, the health worker, and the policemen, boots and all. They'll wreck the black bookshop and the youth opportunity offices. They'll rip up and scatter the sensible shoes and tweed jackets of the social workers. They'll snatch at the cute black girls with their books and high heels and bite up their Asian schoolmates in their multi-coloured saris and linen trousers and rave on in a froth of blood and riot until they get to the groups of Rasta youths lounging about on the other side of the street, and then it will be war.

Apocalyptic thinking, considering it was only just gone lunchtime, but there's something about Birmingham which encourages such fantasies. The Alsatian scrabbled by the side of the Capri and I banged on the inside of the window.

'Shoo, get out of it, ya mangy mutt.'

The snuffling sounds stopped and in a moment I saw the pack padding down the road in front of me. I opened the window a few inches to let out the combined smell of stale perfume and Wally, and wondered when the girls would be back. The last twenty hours or so had passed in what seemed like a flash, and already I was drooping. Train lag. Travel not only broadens the mind, it knackers the body.

The journey had really started on the previous afternoon after Shelagh had left and I'd rung Wally in Wolverhampton.

'Mister Big Time Dean,' he said. 'What you want now?'

We kicked around a few sociable insults for a while, and then I told him about Sara Castle and said I wanted her address.

'You don't want much, do you?'

'You can do it, Wally,' I told him encouragingly.

He could too. Wally was a black photographer I tried to make them hire every time I did a job in the Midlands. He was a freelance and he spent half his time scouring the area for dramatic shots he could sell to the local papers and agencies, trying to repeat the highlight of his career when he'd got some police harassment pics on the front pages of three tabloids.

Sophie sneered at his photos, because the bulk of his trade was concerned with assembling portfolios for black kids trying to get into the beauty trades, and for his sideline he flogged cheapo glamour poses to the tabloids and soft porn mags. Tit and bum Wally she called him, but I'd never been too impressed by the pretensions of the snappers' trade. I usually wanted Wally because he was so useful. His camera, backed up by his smarmily persuasive presence, got him an entry into every nook and cranny of the district, and he had a wide knowledge of the black community and a lot beyond it.

'Well,' he grumbled, after he'd extracted every detail he could think of, 'I'll try.'

He rang me back in about fifteen minutes and gave me the address and phone number.

'Wally,' I said. 'I've got to say it, man. I'm impressed. What did you do?'

'Looked in the phone book.'

Next day, when he met me at New Street station, his face was split by exactly the same complacent grin I'd imagined on the telephone.

'I brought the car,' he said. 'But don't wreck it, and I need it back by six o'clock. I've got choir practice tonight.'

He was a part-time preacher with a beautiful voice and he belonged to a fundamentalist church in the area, where he managed the gospel choir.

On the way he told me what he'd found out that morning.

'The landlord is one of those old Jewish guys who never got out the area. They had the shop on the corner but they sold it to this Asian guy.'

'Who's they?'

'His wife. But she died. They were some kind of Germans or something like that. Been here a long time though.'

'Why you telling me all this stuff about the landlord, man?'

He gave me an indignant glare. His face had grown fatter and rounder and he had acquired a pop-eyed look.

'You always want to know everything.'

I nodded. That was right.

'Anyway,' he continued. 'The girl rented his upstairs last year. She's some kind of probation officer. She gets her papers on the corner. The other one arrived last week. She had to get the keys from Dilip, because the old man was away.'

'What did she look like?'

He gave me a sideways look, and it struck me he was embarrassed.

'It was his wife saw her. She wasn't there. Dilip didn't know. Sorry.'

I stopped at the top of the road to let Wally out. He unbuckled the seat belt, opened the door and turned round.

'The labourer is worthy of his hire.'

We'd agreed on fifty quid. Usually I gave him the money afterwards, but I could see he wanted it right away, and he meant to be heavy about it. When he was really serious he sometimes moved into this Biblical parlance to shade down the confrontation, and, as I usually did, I came back at him in the same language.

'Wally,' I said. 'Though I speak with the tongues of men and of angels, and have not charity, I am become as sounding brass, or a tinkling cymbal.'

I grinned at him, and he sighed, rolled his eyes, and thought for a long moment before he replied.

'Who goeth a warfare any time at his own charges? Who planteth a vineyard, and eateth not of the fruit thereof? Or who feedeth a flock, and eateth not of the milk of the flock?'

He was hitting his stride.

'Whoa,' I said. 'You got it, man.'

I gave him the money, and he counted it carefully and put it away.

'They should have told you at Sunday school,' he said. 'When he said charity he wasn't talking about this stuff. You know what I mean?'

He slammed the door with a flourish and walked jauntily round the corner.

I moved over to the driver's seat, started the car again, fumbling a little with the unfamiliar gears, and continued on down Villa Park Road and then turned off towards the common and the streets backing on to the little stretch of allotments. Once you got into the heart of the area Handsworth had a dignified, elegant look about it, as if the houses had been built for families living gracious lives in a more stately time.

I pulled up in front of Sara's house and sat there looking, trying to work up the energy to do something. It had bow windows at the bottom and long windows opening on to a tiny balcony at the top, but the white paint was now dirty grey and peeling. I'd lived in houses like this years ago, and it reminded me of cleaning out the grate on freezing mornings, fingers numb and aching, crying and cursing under my breath in case my dad heard me.

These weren't memories I wanted, and I dragged my mind angrily round to the present. I could have telephoned Sara from London, but I had thought that might be a waste of time. Besides, if Kim really wanted not to be found, a phone call would simply warn her to get away. That is, if she was with Sara. Even if she wasn't, I'd still have to look into the woman's eyes and convince her I needed her help.

When the dogs reached the next corner I got out of the car, climbed the stairs and rang the top bell. Nothing happened. After I'd rung it a couple more times and waited I gave up and rang the lower one. In a moment there were shuffling noises and the door opened.

The old man had those old-fashioned gold-rimmed glasses with a black ribbon dangling from them. He was wearing a green corduroy suit over a string vest, and he peered through the six-inch gap like a cautious mole. Behind him I could hear the sound of a piano and a voice singing in German.

'What do you want?'

He sounded angry and disgruntled, as if he hadn't spoken to another human being for a while and didn't much want to. He had that aura about him, uninhibited but more or less withdrawn to somewhere else, as if he'd given up his former selves and didn't much care.

I told him that I wanted to see Sara or the girl staying with her, and his expression grew even more forbidding.

'She's out,' he said. 'I don't know anything about them. I don't know.'

The music paused while he stared at me, and started again. I'd been working on it while we talked, and suddenly I got it. As he made to shut the door I raised my finger and looked thoughtfully into his faded blue eyes.

'*Die Rose, die Lilie, die Taube, die Sonne,*' I said slowly.

His head jerked up and a shocked expression crossed his face.

'*Was?*'

'Schumann,' I said. 'Not so?'

'You know this music?'
'Of course.'
He stared at me for a moment, then he smiled widely.
'You are a very strange black man,' he said.

I laughed aloud with real amusement and he heaved up and down in front of me, giving a series of asthmatic grunts which ended in a fit of coughing. When he'd recovered he opened the door wider.

'Come in. Come in. You can wait.'

He showed me into a sitting room which looked like a dusty and run-down antique shop. The furniture, mostly dark and spindly velvet-covered pieces of fragility, choked the room, leaving only narrow passages and islands, where he must have spent his days perching. There were objects everywhere, covering the old flowered wallpaper: pictures, fans, drawings, tiny statuettes and jade pots on the mantelpiece. All of it looked valuable. I sat on a chaise longue covered with a soft plush material. Opposite was an upright piano, lined with photos of the old man, younger but still recognisable, with a dark-haired woman beside him. I looked around openly, hard put to conceal my astonishment.

He watched me with a little smile.

'Junk,' he said. 'All junk. You are a musician?'

He sounded hopeful, and for a moment I wished I was, but I came clean with him.

'My brother studied in Germany,' I told him. 'He lived with a German family and he learned to sing and play the lieder.'

'And he taught them to you?'

He sounded thrilled.

'Yes.'

'Wonderful.'

I didn't tell him that although my brother had liked his former hosts, he'd found almost everything about them extremely funny. He was a brilliant mimic and I'd spent quite a few hilarious hours listening to him taking off their speech and their singing.

He kept shooting sharp little glances at me. I wondered whether he was regretting letting me into his Aladdin's cave, but in a way I wasn't surprised. Most of the whites I encountered thought about black people in rigidly limited categories. Step outside of those and some of them went into a state of mild shock. Once off balance they were credulous and vulnerable. Sometimes it made life easier.

We talked some more. His name was Kurt, and once, long ago, he too had been a student. Not of music. He had not the talent. He made tea and served it, incongruously, in thick white mugs. His wife had played the piano, but now he kept it locked, and in any case he'd lost his voice. He only went to a concert occasionally, ach, he hardly ever went out any more.

After about an hour there was the sound of a key rattling in the outside door. Voices and footsteps went along the passage.

'Your friends,' he said. He sounded annoyed again.

I gave it a minute before I said goodbye, and I heard him locking the door behind me as I climbed the stairs.

Chapter 24

There was no bell, so I knocked on the door. The faint noises in the flat stopped and in a moment the door opened, but the woman standing there was so small that I had to make a conscious adjustment to look down at her.

She had a perky, lively manner and she'd flung open the door with a flourish, as if she was on stage.

'Oh,' she said. 'I thought you were Kurt.'

'I try not to be,' I said.

She shrieked with laughter.

'Did he let you in?' she said when she'd calmed down. 'I didn't hear the bell. Ah. You're the plumber about the bathroom. You must be a new one. You don't look like a plumber.'

She stepped back and waved me into the hallway, talking all the time.

'That's because I'm not,' I said. 'I was waiting with Kurt downstairs. To see you.'

She was moving down the corridor, towards the bathroom I presumed, and when I said this, she stopped in surprise and looked hard at me.

Close up, with her face at rest, it was obvious that she was a grown woman, in her early twenties, but even at a short distance she could have passed for thirteen or fourteen. She had dark brown hair, worn in a pony tail which accentuated the impression of immaturity, and a shrewd little pointed face.

'Waiting with Kurt? Do you know him? He never lets anyone in there.'

'I've got an honest face.'

She talked in a rapid, breathless rush and her conversation leaped from one place to another, like a bird hopping around.

'Well, I don't know about that, but to what do I owe this pleasure?'

'I wish I'd come to see you but it's Kim that I want.'

She raised her eyebrows, and looked round.

'Who are you? What do you want? No one knows she's here.'

'I do,' I said.

She frowned. At a loss.

In the ensuing pause Kim appeared in the door at the end of the hallway. She looked tall beside her friend but I could see she was younger, about twenty-one. She had eyes of the same smoky blue as her mother, but her hair was a lighter shade. It hung down her back in a long plait that reminded me of the way Suzie had been wearing hers, and I wondered for a moment whether there was a connection.

'Who are you? What do you want?'

I took a good look, and now I was the one at a loss. I had been so involved in the search for Kim that I felt I knew her, but face to face with the woman herself I hardly knew what I was going to say.

'I'm Sammy Dean,' I said. 'You've probably heard Aston mention me. I just came to talk to you, about what he was doing lately.'

She stared at me, then her face seemed to crumple and she turned and without a word went back into the room. Sara ran past me, her pony tail flying, and almost immediately I heard Kim crying. Sara had begun speaking to her in a low comforting voice, but I couldn't hear what she was saying.

I stood there for a few minutes, feeling like a beast and wondering what was going to happen. Eventually I went to the open door and looked in. It was a small neat bedroom, probably the spare room. Kim was sitting on the bed with her face in her hands, Sara sat with her arms round her, patting her, and when she heard me at the door she looked round angrily.

'Go away,' she said. 'Just go.'

Kim whispered something I couldn't hear, and Sara turned and leaned closer to her.

'Are you sure?' She swung back to face me. 'Wait a minute. Next door.'

She didn't seem like a child any more. On the contrary, she was operating with a maternal kindness which gave her an odd authority.

I pushed open the door to the right and found myself in a sitting room. It had the same neat look I'd noticed in Kim's place. A sofa, table and chairs, a small CD player, shelves of books. All normal, except for a giant pot plant, which towered to the ceiling, and in that room seemed bizarre and outlandish, like an alien invader.

I hovered a little, then sat at the table and looked at the plant. I couldn't be certain, but it seemed to be growing while I watched, and there was something smirking and arrogant about the way it stood by the window and reached for the sky, which told me it didn't give a damn about whether or not I was observing it.

It was nearly half an hour before they came in. Kim sat on the sofa out of my line of sight, so that I had to look sideways to see her. Sara sat opposite me. They had me covered.

'What is it you want to know?' Sara said.

I told them about Tony being arrested, and I told them I didn't think he'd done it, and that he needed help. No one knew very much, I said, about what Aston had been doing that week, or whether anybody else had a reason for the crime. That was why I wanted to talk to Kim, because I knew she'd been helping Aston. Perhaps she knew more.

'You know who I am,' I told her. 'You know we were friends. He'd have wanted me to do this. To find out what was really happening.'

Sara opened her mouth to speak, but Kim cut in.

'They talked about you when we went to see that old man. Tommy.'

'Yes. Tommy. What did they say?'

She smiled uncertainly.

'They said you were unreliable. They said you never came around.'

Aston had spread that legend about me as assiduously as anyone else. It used to irritate me when I heard him saying it.

'He showed me some articles you'd written. One of them made me laugh. About a writer.'

There was a touch of guilt about that memory. The man's pretensions had irritated me and I'd been mildly ironical at his expense. Later on when I knew more about how such things could hurt, I was sorry.

'That was ages ago.'

She was silent for a few seconds. Her fingers twisted together in her lap. She frowned.

'I don't know what you want me to say.'

'What was Aston up to on the estate?'

'I'm not sure. I hadn't seen him for a little while. We had a sort of argument. But he was always going there.'

'What was the trouble at the youth centre?'

'Oh. Different things. Mostly money. That man who runs it, I can't remember his name.'

'Dalton?'

'Maybe. Something like that. He'd been employing lots of people as youth workers. They weren't qualified and they never did anything. And he'd spent too much on things that didn't happen or just weren't there. Like renovation, new equipment. There were thousands of pounds that couldn't be accounted for. It didn't affect Aston directly but Walter was going to be in big trouble over it.'

'Walter?'

'Yes. He was the secretary or something. He'd signed a lot of cheques without asking about the details. Aston said Walter was frightened of the man. But when it all came out it would look bad for him.'

Ah hah. When Walter talked to me he must have been desperate to start spreading the dirt around. I wondered why he'd changed his mind. Did he think I would do him more damage?

'Was that what you were researching?'

'Oh no. I was looking at contracts and things.'

'In housing?'

'And construction. Mostly.'

'What sort of contracts?'

'It's nothing to do with all this.'

'How do you know? Because it's to do with Marcie?'

'Marcie?'

'She was mostly running housing over the last few years, wasn't she?'

'She wasn't actually in charge most of the time.'

'What was wrong?'

'I can't talk about that.'

Suddenly I was impatient with her. It was true that she was in a bad fix, but she ought to be able to see the implications of the fact that everyone was pointing the finger at only one area.

'Listen, Kim,' I said. 'I don't know whether Aston had an argument with someone over a cigarette packet on the pavement or whether it was to do with his work or what. But the police have this black kid and they're probably working overtime to fit him up. On top of that they're linking the murder to this dodgy business at the youth centre. I mean it's a bit funny that all the lines of enquiry are running straight at black people.'

She turned away from me and shook her head angrily. A gesture, it seemed to me, of denial and rejection.

'What do you think Aston would think about that?'

'I think that's enough,' Sara said hurriedly.

I looked at her and held up my hands in a conciliatory gesture, and she glared back at me with a squint of warning, but she shut up.

'Just one thing,' I said. 'If he was working on anything else at least it would ease the pressure. I don't want to know the details. You don't have to drop anyone in it.'

Bullshit. But I went on quickly before she could think about it.

'For God's sake,' I said. 'We're not the only people who commit crimes. You know what's happening, and it's the usual thing. They're using Aston in a way that would have hurt him if he was still here. I can't believe you want to see that happen.'

'You're just saying that,' Sara burst out. She had that look, offended and somehow stubborn, that I had seen so often in other times, other places. She stared at me resolutely, as if she was ready to fight it out. 'You can't prove that they're wrong, that those people had nothing to do with it. Why does it always have to be something to do with your race?'

I didn't bother to answer her. Instead I gazed at the big plant in the corner. Now that the women were in the room it had lost some of its insolence and acquired a tamer, quieter look.

'Of course it's to do with race,' Kim said. 'I know that much. Aston would have said the same thing.'

She looked straight at me. It gave me an odd feeling and for a moment I had to look away from her before I could meet her gaze. After the day before it was slightly dislocating to see those same sad eyes in her child's face.

'It started with the tenders. Aston said he couldn't find a single instance of Parker & Son's being turned down for a contract. That wasn't altogether peculiar, because they like contractors that they know to be reliable. But recently Parker's had been taking over a lot of the work Direct Labour couldn't do and the tenders weren't low or even average most of the time. Sometimes they were the highest.'

'That's your father's firm.'

She hesitated.

'Yes. Aston was honest about it. He asked if I minded looking up the records. It was delicate because it was my family firm and all the rest of it. He said he thought I'd be fair. I didn't mind. I didn't think there'd be anything much. Besides, I've never agreed with their way of doing things. My dad. Uncle Frank. Politically. They thought the party owed them a living. That was okay in my grandad's day, but they were so racist.

Reactionary. Couldn't stand the changes. I thought that if they got a slap on the wrist they deserved it.'

She looked at the floor, thinking about it. I wondered what her father would have thought about her views, if he'd known. Most young people are astonished and disillusioned by the cynicism and dishonesty of their parents. Not many get the chance to do something about it.

'He came to see me one day. Uncle Frank. He was drunk as usual. My dad drinks a lot but Uncle Frank was like never in his right mind. He said I was breaking my father's heart. A nice Catholic girl, skivvying, taking orders, hanging around a —.' She paused, and drew her breath in hard. 'Hanging around Aston.'

I guessed she wasn't using his precise words.

'I told him to go. But I guess that's how they reacted to my work. I thought it was just how he was. He used to egg my dad on, going on about grandad.'

'What about the tenders?'

'Oh. Well we noticed a few odd things at Kitchener Avenue. It was something stupid. Toilets. Uncle Frank was supplying twice as many toilets as there were houses. We went back over the projects and the budgets always went over, there was a high level of wastage. Nothing you would pick out just like that, but when you added it up over a period of time, it was costing the council an enormous amount of money.'

She was speaking faster, as if reliving the experience of tracking all this down.

'Wait a minute,' I said. 'Wouldn't the auditors have picked all this up?'

'Well, not immediately. That's not the way it works. They would see things bit by bit. They'd begin to get the feel that something was up, but it takes time and investigation to work out what it is. People think of the whole thing as small potatoes, but it can be very complex with an awful lot of money, contracts and all the rest of it going through all the time. Mostly they're seeing that books balance. Even when they know there's something odd they have to be directed to focus attention on it.'

'What about the committees?'

'The officers supervise the requisitions. Receipts, complaints, they'd all go through the departments. Unless someone went out of their way to investigate, they only know what they're told. Besides, you've got to understand. It's highly technical. Difficult. The politics are another thing. Our family has been important down there for years. You'd need to be on pretty firm ground before you started making allegations.'

That being so, it had been clever of Aston to get her to do the groundwork. I wondered whether she'd thought of that, and I wondered how much Aston's liking for her had been influenced by her usefulness. He was a politician after all. But I kicked that thought out of my head as soon as it crept in.

'After a while Marcie worked out what was happening. There was a hell of a row with my dad. We didn't get on very well before, but we haven't spoken to each other since. Aston told me to stop. He said it wasn't fair on me, but he kept on going through the records, and talking to people in the department. I didn't quite know what was happening, but Marcie came to see me last week. She said she knew about us, and she was going to expose him if he didn't pack it in. I think my dad must have sent her. Or Uncle Frank.'

'What did Aston say?'

'We didn't talk about it. I wouldn't have bothered anyway. There were other things on my mind. I just wanted to get away. Not talk to anyone. Then it happened and I came here.'

I thought about what she had told me. I wanted to ask her the next obvious question, and I didn't know quite how to put it. But she was ahead of me.

'I couldn't have been the only one who knew,' she said. 'It stopped being a big secret a while ago. Everyone in the departments knew Aston was trying to sort out the Parkers. I know what you're thinking but it's a lot more complicated than that. If you looked at it the way we did it was obvious what was going on, but there wasn't anything you could take into court and convict people with, you see. At the most it was a kind of negligence in the civic centre, and sharp practice at

Parker's. Some people would say it was good business and Aston was being spiteful.'

Sara gave a sarcastic bark, and Kim shrugged despairingly.

'So what was it all about? Why did Aston bother?'

'He wanted to stop them. The issue was credibility. Everyone knew the Parkers had things sewn up, and my dad, Kevin, Uncle Frank, their power's all tied up with that. If Aston had a clear enough picture to convince the committee and the council all that would go down the drain. But it was all getting late in the day. The selection's going on now. The voting starts next week. Once Aston had been selected, if he hadn't got an investigation going they'd have to leave it till after the election. Too risky washing dirty linen then.'

He must have been desperate to complete his strategy of undermining Parker before having to leave, I thought. Sara got up and looked at me.

'Cup of tea?'

I nodded and she went over to Kim and put a hand on her shoulder.

'You all right?'

Kim smiled up at her wanly.

'Mmm.'

I watched Sara go out of the room. Through the open door I could hear her banging about. I had the feeling that the convolutions Kim had been describing were too much for her and she'd wanted to escape. On the other hand, I was thinking that all this was a more credible motive for getting rid of Aston than anything I'd heard so far.

'I know what you're thinking,' Kim said. Her eyelids were red and puffy, and her face was pink and flushed, so that she looked younger, even more vulnerable. I felt the urge to pat her on the head and reassure her, everything would be all right. I suppressed it. She might look like a child but she had a subtle and powerful brain, and I could see how she and Aston would have made a formidable team.

'I know how it would look to an outsider,' she said. 'But they wouldn't harm Aston. It was a sort of game. Whoever made the right moves could win, and they had a lot of advantages. Aston couldn't risk rocking the boat just before the election. With all the loony Left business, no Labour seat is really safe the way it used to be. The youth centre scandal couldn't be hushed up and it was going to be damaging enough. Throw in something like a new corruption investigation and there would be a real danger of losing. Aston was almost certain to get the selection and win the seat. So his hands were tied for months.'

'What about after the election? The problems weren't going to go away.'

She stopped and Sara came back in carrying a tray. Kim looked up with what seemed like relief. Sara put the tray down quietly as if trying not to disturb us, and began pouring the tea.

'I'm pregnant,' Kim said.

Sara's hand shook and she spilled a little tea into my saucer. I looked up and she was watching me fiercely, as if daring me to say something.

'By the time of the election it would be showing. You don't suppose anyone missed the significance of that fact.'

I could imagine. Kim was a young convent-reared girl from a solid Catholic family. Aston had been her employer, nearly twice her age, and black. The hoo-ha would have been enormous.

'Oh. As an MP he would have survived all the fuss and by the time the next reselection came up the publicity would have died down. But locally, a lot of people would have seen my father as the injured party, and even if they supported Aston as a politician, when it came down to accusing Parker & Son of a fiddle, most of them would bend over backwards to avoid taking sides. Aston wouldn't have stood a chance of proving my dad had been fixing things. So you see, all they had to do was wait and the problem would be solved. There was no need to hurt Aston.'

Sara picked up her cup and went over to Kim with it. She was standing between us, so I couldn't see exactly what happened, but suddenly Kim put the cup on the floor sharply enough to spill half of it, and then she was up and flying to the door, the plait at the back of her head swinging with every step. Sara called out loudly, but Kim didn't turn round or pause. In a moment we heard a door slam. That was it, I guessed.

Chapter 25

'Sorry,' I told Sara.

She was still staring at the door, and when I spoke she looked round absently.

'Never mind, it's not your fault.'

I knew that, but everything I'd thought about Kim had changed. In spite of her divided loyalties and the power-hungry factions fighting over her body she had managed things with dignity and integrity. No one could blame her for wanting to get away from it all.

'Thanks for your hospitality,' I said. 'I'm off now.'

She stared at me, biting her lip as if trying to make up her mind about something.

'Hang on a minute,' she said eventually. 'I'll walk down with you.'

She went out and I heard her go into Kim's room. The time seemed to stretch out interminably and after several minutes I was making up my mind to leave when she came out and stood waiting for me in the hallway.

'Come on then,' she said.

We went down to the door and instead of leaving me there as I expected she came out, shut the door behind her and walked beside me down to the pavement.

'Is this your car?' she asked when she saw the Capri.

'Nope. I borrowed it.'

'That's good. You don't look like one of those. I'd have had to change all my ideas about you.'

Now we were outside she had recovered her perkiness, and I had the feeling she'd have been much happier with the light teasing conversation we'd started. But there was something on her mind and she was only putting off what she had really had to say.

'There isn't an easy way to say this,' she told me. 'I'm not convinced by all that racism business, but there was something you ought to know. She can't tell you herself, but she knows what I'm saying. She trusts you. But this could hurt a lot of people, especially her. So you've got to promise not to tell anyone at all. She'll deny it if you do.'

'What is it?'

'Something she told Aston. Do you promise?'

'Yes. I promise.'

She looked around at the windows of the house. I looked up too, but there was no one there. Two young dreadlocks came past. One of them nodded his head at me and I raised my hand. She pursed her lips and waited until they were out of earshot.

'The monster, her father,' she said, 'abused her when she was a kid.'

'What?'

'Get in the car.'

We got into the car. I wound my window down and looked at her.

'It happened when she was twelve, thirteen, when she was at school. She couldn't tell, but she made him stop later on. The first person she talked to about it was me, at college. She had a bad time, partly because of that, and she dropped out. I think afterwards she sort of came to terms with it. Anyway, she told Aston when she knew about the baby. She wanted him to know everything about her. The thing is, if Aston had tried to use it ...'

'Anything could happen.'

'Yes.'

'Is that what she thinks?'

'No.' She sounded shocked. 'If she thought Aston did that it would kill her.'

I didn't think it would but I could see what she meant.

'Does her mother know?'

'Of course not. She mustn't. He hates them both. He bashes her mother when he feels like it. But he's scared of Kim, in case she says anything. I think that's why she was helping Aston in the first place. To get back at him.'

The man was probably in a state of spiritual anguish and mental turmoil. Perhaps lashing out at everyone helped.

'I must go back,' she said. 'Remember you promised.'

'I'll remember,' I said.

Chapter 26

The doorbell ringing woke me. As if the horrible insistent jangling wasn't enough, there was someone groaning loudly in the room, and I was just about to get angry at their lack of consideration when I realised that it was me.

I lay still trying to blank out the penetrating noise of the bell. But the torture didn't stop, and in the end I rolled out of bed, blundered to the window, pushed about a foot of it open and stuck my head through.

My son was standing on the pavement below looking up. The sight cleared my brain like a dash of cold water in the face. The school uniform gave him an unfamiliar adult look, the tie carelessly knotted, the collar that tiny bit askew.

'Dad,' he shouted. 'Open the door, Dad.'

I stumbled down the stairs, literally sliding and falling on the last flight. When I opened the door he was looking at me with an air of mingled concern and irritation.

'What took you so long, Dad?'

'Never mind what took me so long. What time is it?'

I was scuttling back upstairs as fast as I could go.

'Eight o'clock.'

'Oh my God.'

In the kitchen he viewed me with a disapproving eye while I put the kettle on. I'd noticed it before, but this morning there seemed to be something more than normally puritanical about him, like a beautiful and stern young sergeant major about to crush a particularly unsavoury private.

'Why didn't you answer the phone, Dad?'

That was easy enough. I had missed one train from Brum, walked down the road to a pub in the Bull Ring, and missed the next one. The one I eventually caught was a slow one which didn't get me back to London until after midnight. Then I didn't have enough money for a taxi and I had to walk home. I'd been in a sort of waking dream, my mind churning with what I'd learnt that day, and just as I'd begun to doze off the phone had rung. A drunken Scottish voice asking for Dawn. I'd slammed it down and when it rang again, I'd taken it off the hook and left it.

'So aren't you going to tell me what's the matter? Why aren't you at school?'

'I'm on my way. I came to see you first.'

The police had rung up late last night, he said, asking for me. They'd said to tell me to get in touch. Since then he'd been trying to reach me.

'A man with a funny name. I wrote it down.'

'Borelli?'

'That's it. My mum said you must be in some kind of trouble.'

Damn and blast her, and damn and blast Borelli. I'd kill him for this.

'Look son. Don't you remember me talking about Borelli? Guy I was at school with? He was a dummy and he became a copper. We used to fight in the playground. He was one of those.'

'Oh yeah. He sounded okay on the telephone. I didn't remember.'

'Okay. He probably wants to speak to me. Go out for a drink, or a little punch up behind the station toilets. Just try and remember things before you panic.'

He looked a little dubious but I was there in front of him, pouring a cup of tea. Everything must be all right. He cheered up.

'Wasn't me, Dad. I didn't think you'd done anything. But my mum looked sort of worried and it scared me.'

I shook my head. Now it was over he was grinning, relieved. I looked at him over my tea cup. The poor little devil must have had a night of terror and his first thought in the morning had been to be with me. I felt sad and elated at the same time. Love.

'I even rang that Maman Nightingale,' he said. 'But they didn't know anything.'

'Well they wouldn't, would they?' How did you get the number?'

He grinned. Dead superior.

'I know they've all got names like that back home, Dad, but it's not so common in this country. She was the only one in that street in the phone book.'

So bright. He was relaxed now.

'That dressing gown, Dad. I mean. Dad, man. Where'd you get a dressing gown like that?'

This was going too far. My quilted Italian dressing gown, cut Japanese style. My pride and joy.

'That's quite enough of that, old son,' I told him. 'Off to school.'

As soon as he'd gone I rang Borelli. When he answered I asked him who the hell he thought he was, scaring my family like that.

'Calm down,' he said. 'I was only trying to do you a favour. Get in touch with you. I never said anything out of order, man.'

He was right and everyone had over-reacted. I'd noticed it before. Policemen and women often forgot that their mere presence could cause alarm, and then they'd try and behave like normal people. Come round and see you. Telephone. No idea.

'Okay. Okay. What's up?'

'Your mate. Walter Davis. Chucked himself out of a window last night.'

'What?'

'Yeah, I've been up all night. Can you come round the station? I'm hearing that the two of you were as thick as thieves the last week or so. I want to know what's going on.'

'What's going on?'

My tongue didn't seem to be working properly. Never mind my tongue, my brain was reeling with shock.

'Come off it. Uckin' Sammy Dean. Don't give me grief, man. Just come down the station.'

'What time?'

His voice took on an exaggeratedly casual note.

'I'm having a press conference in a couple of hours. I want to talk to you before that.'

'Press conference, eh? Big shot.'

'If you got it,' he said. 'Flaunt the bugger. Right? Get down here.'

He rang off. I rang Aubrey and told him about Walter.

'I know,' he said. 'It was on the radio.'

'Were you round there last night?'

'No. I was round my sister's.'

'I'm not interested in your alibi, man. I just want to know if you know what's going on.'

He laughed.

'No. But I'll take a walk down there today and check it.'

I put the phone down and I'd just turned away when it rang again.

'Peter.'

'Peter? Peter who?'

'Wake up, Sammy. I've been trying to get you all morning.'

Peter news editor. That's who.

'Okay. You got me. I am Sammy Dean and all you have to do is answer one simple question and claim your crisp new fiver.'

'Very good, Sammy. I'll laugh when I've had a drink. Have you heard about this Walter Davis business?'

'Yes.'

'Have you been down there?'

Typical. He thought it was totally normal to rush off to the scene of a violent death.

'I'm on my way.'

'Good. You wrote the piece about Aston. It looks like there's something going on down there. Go and have a look, will you?'

I felt a twinge of irritation. Not about the way he was ordering me about. That was just part of his professional persona. It was the familiar way he referred to Aston that got me. Deskmen like Peter spent the entire day in the office and then went home, but they talked about politicians and other famous people they'd never met as if they were old drinking buddies. Aston, Ken, Neil, Edwina.

'What do you want?'

'I dunno. Use your judgement. Get on the estate and look behind the scenes. They've got pushers, they're investigating the youth centre, Aston was killed there, now this Walter Davis thing. The tabloids are calling it the death estate. If you can, find some solid stuff linking things up . . .'

He left the sentence unfinished, but I could imagine what he was after.

'You must have some people there.'

'Sure. But we could do with your special talents, Sammy.'

He meant that an ageing black street punk like me would find out more than the white Oxbridge boys and girls on the staff.

'There's a press conference, but I wouldn't bother too much about that. The police are trying to play things down. They're denying there's any connection between the two deaths. Go down and call me when you know what things look like. About twoish?'

'Okay.'

I got dressed and started out for the nick to see Borelli. It was about nine, and I felt an undertone of annoyance at being caught in the rush hour. I didn't mind being up and around earlier or later, but I had a continual sense that at least one compensation for my way of life was that I didn't have to struggle along with the rest of the punters.

Things were humming at the station. There was a radio van parked in front and, dwarfing it, two outside broadcast TV trucks. Inside, a camera team was hanging around fiddling with their equipment, and two young women wearing jeans, clipboards and smug expressions were walking back and forth ordering people about.

As I crossed the lobby a black youth was being led through in front of me flanked by a couple of policemen, and all three of them turned to stare at the TV circus with exactly the same mixture of open-mouthed astonishment and hostility.

I went up to the desk sergeant, the same man I'd seen before, and I told him who I was and asked for Borelli. He nodded, opened a flap in the counter and led me through. We went along a narrow corridor, then up a flight of stairs and along another corridor to a glass-fronted office where Borelli was sitting behind a desk. He got up and shook hands with me, waved me to a seat, and turned to the sergeant.

'Cup of tea, John?'

His behaviour astonished me. Borelli had always been a lout, but now someone seemed to have taught him manners. Then it struck me that here in the station with the press hovering, he was not only practising a more up-market style. He was also demonstrating himself to be a sophisticated senior man.

'What's it all about, Sammy?'

'More or less what I told you before.'

I told him about Walter coming to see me and how I'd been down the estate with him, gone to see him at the civic centre, and how he'd withdrawn his co-operation only the other day.

'I suppose it's natural,' Borelli said, grinning. 'You can be a right pain in the ass.'

I didn't dignify that with any comment, and just then a policewoman came in with two big white mugs.

'Tea,' Borelli bellowed. 'Deirdre, you're amazing my love.'

I watched him cynically. This was his version of keeping the team happy.

'I think the Parkers were putting pressure on him,' I said, when she'd gone.

'Suppose it was someone else. What about this bloke Dalton? Fancied himself, didn't he? Old Walter was the secretary of their little set-up. Just suppose he was going to grass them up?'

'Come off it, Borelli. It wasn't that big a deal. Besides, I thought you said he chucked himself out the window.'

'Do you know where it was?'

'No.'

'It was an empty flat on the tenth floor. The neighbours heard an argument going on shortly before he went out the window. They took no notice, of course, there's always something going on in these empty places. Crack dealers break in and use them. People mind their own business. The funny thing was that he was down there littering the bloody pavement a long time, ten, fifteen minutes, before anyone found him. It was late and that's the quiet side. Whoever was with him had plenty of time.'

'So what is it, apart from it being on the estate, that makes you think it's something to do with Dalton?'

'Mate of yours, is he?'

I stared at him steadily, and he stared back.

'Same as you,' I said.

Suddenly he grinned triumphantly. All over his face.

'I'm going to let you have this,' he said, 'ahead of your pals out there.'

Fifteen minutes at this time of day was nothing at all, and he knew it.

'The last place Walter Davis was seen,' he said sonorously, 'was at the youth centre, talking to your mate Dalton, and he pissed off pretty sharpish, because when we went looking for him in the early hours he'd disappeared and he hasn't been seen since. We've got a warrant out for him. We want him to help us with our enquiries.'

He gave me a cute look with the last bit.

'That's your evidence?'

'I'm not saying he's done it. We just want to ask him a few questions. Like what they were talking about and why he went into hiding before Davis hit the ground.'

'Same questions you asked me, Franco.'

He looked at me seriously, and with a hint of anger. All humour gone.

'Listen, Sammy. Don't take the piss. If I didn't know you, you wouldn't be sat here scoffing tea. You know what I mean?'

The press conference was as dramatic as Borelli and his cohorts could make it. Which really wasn't all that.

On the other hand, there was a kind of tension in the room which came mostly from the mass of notebook burns. Not many had known Walter, but all of them knew what it is to hustle from job to job, worry about the rent, drink too much and wind up in some shit hole of a local newsroom or cleaning up the mess behind a big-headed bunch of small-time politicos. Somewhere in their instincts they were feeling the uneasiness that came from identifying with bits of his life, and somewhere in there too, they were mourning him as one of themselves. Life's a bitch and then you die.

The atmosphere washed by the young smoothies from the TV, on a wobbly parabola between graduation ceremony and stardom. This was a minor local story and they studied their notes and scribbled their thirty-second scripts with a studied ostentation.

But it was to them that Borelli was primarily addressing himself. He read a statement outlining the circumstances of Walter's death, and said that the police weren't yet treating this as a murder enquiry. Then he told them that he wanted to interview Dalton. He held up a picture, and gave them a few selected highlights of Dalton's career. The scribbling became furious when Borelli said he was a graduate of the local polytechnic.

Next he took the questions. Non-committal about any links between Walter and the investigation into Aston's death or the investigation into the youth centre finances. He let himself go a bit on drugs, then it was over, and Borelli stalked out looking like a cross between Sherlock Holmes and Inspector Gideon.

I picked up one of the pictures. It was a blow-up of a snap taken on the street somewhere. He looked hard and touchy. A dangerous man.

At the door I bumped into one of Peter's toughies. She had

straggly brown hair, wore specs and looked like a village schoolteacher. She gave me a sharp, suspicious glance.

'Hello, Sammy,' she said. 'Peter said you'd be here. I thought you were doing background.'

That meant – leave the press conference stuff alone.

'I am,' I said. 'I just nipped in to see what was going on.'

She looked reassured and asked me for some local directions. She followed that by telling me that if I ran into any witnesses who hadn't come forward or anyone with a good quote about last night's events she wanted to know right away. Then she lost interest in me and pushed off.

The rest of the day I spent mostly talking to various people on the estate. I dropped in on a couple I knew vaguely, and they sent me along to another family I knew. No one knew anything about the deaths but they had a lot to say about Dalton and the youth centre. Everyone I talked with viewed them, to one degree or another, as a threat and a nuisance. A young boy or girl who went down that centre would be sure to get into trouble sooner or later. And the crack. My friends who spoke about it lowered their voices. Don't talk. It was terrible.

Early in the afternoon I rang Peter. I had no news, so I had to box clever. But it was a quality paper, which gave me a bit of leeway.

I told him I didn't have anything specific along the lines we'd talked about. He groaned, and I pointed out that I knew Borelli, the bill in charge, and I'd had a private interview with him. I said that I thought the police evidence so far was rubbish and Dalton was mainly in trouble because he was a central focus for the troubles and tensions on the estate. He perked up at that and I said Walter was a good peg for a feature about the conditions on the estate which focused on the way that residents felt about the failures of the local administration and police.

'All right,' he said, 'give us a thousand words and I'll play about with it.'

I put the phone down smiling. Peter was shrewd, but I knew by now what he'd go for, and this was exactly what I'd planned to do before I left the flat that morning.

I dropped in on Eva before I went back home. She greeted me with a nervous smile. She looked thinner and a little haggard.

In the back Granny shushed us as we went in. She was watching a soap opera on telly, her eyes glistening like little wet beads, and though she said hello to me her attention never swerved.

'This Dalton business. How do you think it looks for Tony?' Eva asked.

'Better, rather than worse,' I told her.

On the screen a red-haired woman in a spectacularly ugly flowered dress was telling a blonde woman with a look of painful sympathy on her face that she had really fallen for that rat. Granny cackled with sarcastic amusement, and Eva's eyes shifted to the telly. I had the feeling that the moment I was gone she would be sitting beside Granny, transfixed.

I told her that chasing after Dalton gave the police something else to concentrate on. People were linking Aston's death with Walter's and that let Tony off the hook to some extent. The more complex and confusing the situation was, the safer Tony would be.

I was making all this up as I went along but she seemed convinced. I didn't stay for the cup of tea she offered me, because I felt that I was interrupting a familiar ritual and that both women would be quite pleased to see me out of the way.

Chapter 27

I picked up Aubrey on the corner of the Harrow Road near the police station where we'd arranged to meet on the telephone. At the time it had struck me that this was something he didn't want Maman to know about, but when I began asking him about it, his tone had been curt and preoccupied, quite unlike his normal manner.

'Don't waste time asking questions,' he said. 'Just come.'

He was smiling as usual when he slid into the seat next to me, but there was an unfamiliar undertone of tension.

'What's up?'

'Tell you in a minute,' he said. 'Make a right and go on up by Swiss Cottage.'

I moved off, and I was so affected by the way he was behaving that as I did so I glanced round over my shoulder to see if any police cars were coming out of the yard.

'It's Dalton,' Aubrey said. 'We're going to see him.'

'What?'

'He wants to see you.'

'Wait a minute, Aubrey. How does he even know I know you?'

He looked at me sideways.

'I told them guys. I told them you were checking this police jinnal and you could get him off. I said you wanted to see him.'

In my state of shock I nearly stopped the car.

'Why the hell did you do that, man?'

'One or two knew about you. And me. I had to say something.' He paused. 'Besides you've got to see him, haven't you?'

'Sure, but why'd you say I could get him off?'

He grinned at me.

'Don't worry. Nobody believed it. I reckon the guy's got a reason he wants to see you.'

When we got through Swiss Cottage he directed me round a couple of corners and we drew up in front of a semi in a quiet street.

'You sure this is the place?'

'Yeh. Is some kind of rich woman.'

'He knows we're coming?' I didn't fancy any misunderstandings with Dalton.

'Sure.'

The woman who opened the door was fortyish, tall and thin, with gold-rimmed glasses and a blond page boy cut. She looked respectable, prosperous, and a bit of an intellectual. Just what you'd expect halfway up Haverstock Hill.

'You're Mister Dean?'

'That's right,' I said. I'd been feeling pretty disorientated, and now I was almost tongue-tied with shock.

If she noticed she paid no attention, merely turning and leading the way through the hallway to a room which ran the depth of the house and looked out on to a big overgrown garden. There was a piano in one corner and a music stand with a cello case lying next to it. Against the wall facing the door was a pot big enough to stand on the floor, covered with an intricate pattern of tiny blue flowers. The French windows were open, and Dalton was sitting in an armchair viewing the garden as if he didn't have a care in the world. When we came in he laughed, waved and gestured at the sofa near him. The lady of the house smiled politely.

'Would you like some tea?'

I said yes. Aubrey hesitated.

'Could I have some juice please?'

She gave us the hostess smile again and turned to go. Then she swung back to me.

'My name's Victoria, by the way. Tory. Dalton has no manners at all.'

Dalton laughed as if he was used to hearing this and enjoyed it. Tory shook her head in mock reproof and went on out. When she'd gone I looked round at the line of abstract paintings on the wall. They seemed to provide a precise echo of what I was feeling.

'I wish I was wanted by the police,' I said. 'You're doing all right.'

Dalton laughed.

'Tory is my old spa. We had a heavy thing when I was a young boy and we been friends ever since. She's a real friend, you know how I mean?'

I knew. Dangerous charismatic men should always count on the unquestioning loyalty of at least one woman, and probably quite a few more.

He laughed again.

'Anyway, I'm giving myself up tomorrow. They're only trying to fit me up. They've got no case. But it might take a while to get out. I want a couple of days to do some things before I go in.'

He didn't say what the things were, and I decided against asking. I didn't want to know.

'Where do I come in?'

'Seems like you doing some investigation. I heard about you. Checked you out. You been around. I don't think they can get me on this thing but once I go in I'll need all the help I can get.'

I couldn't argue with that.

'Walter,' he went on. 'There's some connection with this Aston business. When I talked to him yesterday he said he knew who did it.'

He watched me seriously and when I registered a sufficient degree of shock he nodded.

'Yes. I think he might have told the wrong people.'

Tory came back in with a tray, which held a delicate teapot with a tiny wildflower pattern and matching cups. I almost stood up when she came into the room. Aubrey did and, with a courteous air, took the tray and helped her lay out the tea things. Dalton, taking his ease in the armchair, watched us fussing around her with a wide grin.

'You should check out who Walter talked to,' he said when she'd gone.

'Any suggestions?'

He spread his hands.

'I don't know. Some of them Labour Club people?'

That wasn't a big help and he had the grace to look apologetic.

'Was that why Walter came to see you?'

'No. He just mentioned that. He wanted support for the nomination.'

'The nomination. Isn't that too late?'

'No. Some of the branches haven't voted on their shortlists. And even when all of them have, the general committee can still shortlist who the hell they like for the final beauty contest. But he wanted to sew up our branch, and he wanted me to talk to some of the black people in the others.'

'But the other candidates, they must have been too far ahead, surely?'

'I don't know. Depends on who you've got. Walter would have got most of the black people. But that wouldn't be enough. He said the Parkers and their people were supporting him. They were putting his name up, and jacking up the union people.'

'Why? I thought Kevin was their man.'

'That's what I thought,' he said, 'but he was pretty sure he had them. That was Walter, too damn smart for his own good. Find out what he had on them.'

The blithe way he talked about finding out these things got on my nerves. I was already knocking myself out trying to find out things half the borough knew.

I asked him whether he had any hints about where Walter was going when he'd left and he shook his head impatiently. I suspected that I'd learnt all that I was going to from him.

'Aren't you taking a chance? Bringing people here. Coming here yourself.'

He stared at me, then broke into his laugh.

'Chance? No chance at all. Only a couple of people know, and who's going to talk? You?'

He had a point.

'On top of that, look around you. Police don't trouble people like this. And the next thing is, if a police walk in here right now, Tory would just say good evening.' He did a passable imitation of her manner. 'Then she'd introduce me and the sucker still wouldn't recognise me. Prejudice make them stupid, man. I'm in the wrong place. If I was hiding out in a squat in Brixton they'd get me in about half an hour, but here I can stay as long as I like. I'm safe.'

Chapter 28

I kept telling myself that there must have been more questions I could have asked Dalton, but I couldn't imagine what they were.

As we went down through Swiss Cottage towards Paddington Aubrey looked at me curiously.

'Any good?' he asked me eventually.

I shrugged. 'Let me ask you a question. Can you imagine that Parker backing a black man for the selection?'

'No way.' Aubrey shook his head emphatically.

'Right. So if Walter thought he was going to back him it was because he had a good reason, like Walter had something on him. You follow me? And that something had to be real serious.'

'Aston?'

'Right.'

That didn't seem a particularly penetrating bit of deduction, so we kicked it around some more trying to figure out what kind of evidence Walter had and how he'd got on to it, but by the time we reached Maman's house we hadn't worked any of it out.

I didn't go in because I wanted to make a quick dash to Sophie's place. It was past ten, but if she was in we could go for a meal or fish and chips maybe, and I could talk to her about some of the things that had been happening.

I drove back north through St John's Wood, round Lords and up the side of Regent's Park. In the dark the trees looked immense, shapeless, and even through the noise of the engine I could hear them sighing and whistling.

There was something mournful about the sound which set me to remembering Aston. I'd wanted to see him succeed, to show him off to my son, so he could feel and share the pride I felt for this friend of my childhood. Walter too. I'd stopped liking him, but it was true that he'd become a substantial man. I had thought that sometime I would tell my son about how Walter had come to see me at the start of his career, and then I could say that he wasn't my cup of tea, but look how well he'd done.

Now both of them had been killed, same as any squabbling street corner yardie boy, and in these circumstances there was nothing good about being dead. You couldn't use it as an example of civic and moral virtue or paint glowing pictures about such a person's industry and determination. In any case, when you died you were dead, and there was the end of it. That's the trouble with dead people. They're all the same.

I wondered whether Sophie would understand or share my thoughts. Over the last week I'd been listening to other people, trying to uncork their secrets, cueing my responses to theirs and bending my will into a persuasive instrument. Now I wanted to talk about what I felt: to be myself.

There was a light on in the studio and I went up the stairs quickly. At the back of my mind I kept hoping she would be alone and in a good mood, but when she answered the bell I could tell immediately that she was neither.

She was wearing a short cotton bathrobe which had been a promotional gift from a hotel chain in Florida, and the way she stood in front of me holding it wrapped around herself gave everything away.

'Oh. Sammy,' she said. 'I've got company.'

Osvaldo flashed through my mind. Inside me was a numb, icy feeling, and somewhere behind it a sparkling glow of anger.

'So? I don't mind,' I said. 'I can see it's an informal occasion.'

She stared at me for a moment, then her eyebrows lifted and her mouth twisted in a resigned grimace. She turned and led the way back into the flat. I closed the door and followed her.

'You want some coffee?'

We were going to be urbane. Might as well relax.

'Yes.'

Now my first reaction was past I was thinking about Marcie and Shelagh. I hadn't intended to tell Sophie about any of that and I still wasn't going to. But what had happened with them seemed to give the situation an uneasy balance. Whatever she did with Osvaldo couldn't be much different. It was, I supposed, a sort of justice, and I would surprise her by accepting the situation.

'Who is it?' I muttered. As if I didn't know.

She gave a silent chuckle, shook her head, and made a helpless gesture with both hands up in front of her as if all this was too much and she'd given up.

I went into the studio. Now it was here I was almost eager for the confrontation, and it was a shock to see a woman climbing backwards down the steps, a sheet clasped awkwardly about most of her. She reached the bottom, looked round, and I recognised Spid.

In her turn she gave me a startled look, and clutched the sheet tighter around her.

'Is this him? Your bloke?' she said to Sophie who had come in behind me.

Sophie made an odd sound and when I looked round I saw that she was doubled up with laughter. In spite of everything I found myself grinning at her. The truth was that I felt relieved, and after the tension I'd been feeling I didn't find it hard to share her amusement. But in a moment she straightened up, repeated that gesture with both her hands and went off into the kitchen. I turned back to face Spid, still standing at the foot of the steps, draped in her sheet. Her chin tilted aggressively at me and her expression was defiant. The whole ensemble gave her the air of a heroic statue.

'What are you going to do?' she said. 'Beat me up?'

I thought this was another one of her sarcasms but the unflinching way she stood staring told me that she was half expecting me to do just that, and even though the persistence of her hostility irritated me I felt a twinge of something like respect.

'Don't be stupid,' I said. 'What goes on between Sophie and anyone else is her business.'

That was the line I'd decided on.

'I don't want to know,' I said, 'but I still want to talk to you about Aston. I don't know why you decided I was trying to get gossip on you, but if you look in the paper tomorrow you'll see a serious piece by me that doesn't mention you.'

'I know,' she said. 'I saw the article about Aston yesterday.'

She didn't apologise.

'All right,' I said. 'There's still a lot going on and there's a couple of things I need to know.'

I sat down on the far side of the table, so that she wouldn't feel threatened, and, as if on cue, Sophie came back into the room with the coffee. Spid let the sheet fall and walked over to the armchair where her clothes were lying, neatly folded. I'd only ever seen her in a loose shirt and baggy trousers and somehow I'd expected her naked body to look equally baggy, but she had a chunky athletic figure with firm small breasts and tight hard thighs.

Now the explanations were over she seemed calm and unselfconscious, not at all worried about her nudity or about getting dressed in front of me. She slipped her sweater over her head and pulled on her trousers, then came to the table, sat down, picked up her coffee and smiled at Sophie, who smiled back.

'I don't really see the point,' she said. 'I can't tell you much more than you already know.'

She didn't smile at me.

'I don't know whether that's true or whether you're just saying that,' I said. 'You know Walter's dead?'

She nodded her head.

'Yes. I heard it on the radio. It was an accident or something.'

'I think he was pushed,' I said.

I told her I'd talked to someone who'd seen Walter the day before. I didn't tell her it was Dalton. She'd had enough surprises. But when I told her what Walter had said about knowing Aston's killer, she frowned uneasily.

'It all goes back to whatever Aston was working on,' I told her. 'It's all very well you keeping schtumm but there's two connecting threads. One is the estate, the other is the town hall. The cops are going to work on the estate because they've got two black people to lay it on and it's easier and more sexy and nobody's going to lean over the chief at the next Masonic dinner and ask him what the hell is going on. And if you all keep your mouths shut it will all go right through the way it's going now.'

I'd chosen my angle with care. In spite of her position she had a deep-seated belief in the general malevolence of the state and all its agents and she wouldn't want to be lined up on their side. I could see that she was beginning to waver.

'Whatever you tell me,' I said solemnly, 'will remain confidential. I promise never to use it without your permission and as soon as I work out what's going on I'll forget you ever told it to me.'

'You can believe him,' Sophie said. 'He means it.'

Spid made up her mind in a couple of seconds.

'There was an investigation going on. I didn't know about it right away because I had an argument with Aston and we hadn't been talking beyond saying hello.'

'What was the row about?'

Her eyes flicked towards Sophie, and she took a little while before she replied.

'About that girl. I thought he was messing her around, and I told him so. Men can be beastly.'

'I can't believe you said that,' I told her, and she frowned at me.

'Sammy,' Sophie said in a tone of admonishment. 'Go on,' she said encouragingly to Spid.

Now she was like this, backing me up and trying to help, it was hard to remember that things weren't going well between us.

'He phoned me one night, and he came round. The internal audit had picked up something dodgy involving Parker's firm. In three years or so, they hadn't missed a single tender they'd gone after. On the actual jobs they overran the budgets, and there was always enough wastage to support two or three contractors. They weren't the only ones on the elbow, but they kept coming up again and again and they were costing us a hell of a lot of money. We're talking about millions, right?'

'How were they getting away with it?'

'That was the problem. Have you ever worked in local government?'

'No.' I didn't add thank God, although it was on the tip of my tongue.

'Well, there's stuff going on all the time. There's small fiddles like stores, equipment and material going walkies. Then there's bigger things, people selling favours, and the really big ones, involving a number of people and a lot of money. The bigger they are, the more subtle and difficult to prove they become.'

I met her eyes seriously, struggling with a sense that all this was unreal. A short while ago she'd been climbing stark naked out of Sophie's bed, ready to mix it with me. Now she was talking with the grave air of an expert, and I was listening to her with an increasing feeling of respect. To make matters worse, I was sure that she was keeping it simple, and I couldn't even object to her patronising me. I needed it simple.

I concentrated. All this had happened a few months ago, shortly after Aston took over the chair of construction services. Given Parker's position in the branch and the district it was delicate. In the normal way of things the chair would have met with the council's Leader and a few other key members and got the ball rolling. But that was also the point at which rumours would begin to get out, and people could start moving to bury the evidence or bury the investigation.

'You'd be surprised,' she said, 'how many of these cases get sidetracked or the evidence simply falls apart when it gets to the point.'

'So what did he do?'

She grimaced, as if she didn't quite approve of what he'd done.

'Well, he had to find out what was actually going on. It's not like the old days you give someone a contract because you like them. That went out in the sixties. It's technical now. To get these tenders right they needed inside information about the way the bids were shaping up. Get that and you can beat the competition every time, but you need quantity surveyors, architects maybe. But it was the quantity surveyor's office. Had to be.'

She paused and squinted at the table, considering.

'More coffee?' Sophie asked.

She sounded respectful and a little subdued. Spid smiled at her and nodded, looking her in the eyes as she got up.

'You too, Sammy?'

I said yes, but I was busy thinking about the way they'd looked at each other. In the last few minutes Spid had suddenly turned into a more substantial person than I'd imagined, and perhaps what had happened between her and Sophie was more serious than I'd thought.

'The other part of the scam,' Spid said, 'was in the supervision. The trouble is the budgets have huge margins. You can't lay out everything at the beginning. Things go wrong. There are disputes. Problems emerge. Unless your quantity surveyors have a careful grip on specifications it can get out of control. If your surveyor's office is bent you've had it. People can simply not do the work they're being paid for, or they can over-purchase and flog off the extra. Regular little business.'

I leaned back in my chair struggling to keep my attention on what she was saying. High over her shoulder I could see the moon, hanging just above the glass panes of the ceiling, an almighty silver globe. On a good night I could be lying in bed with Sophie looking at it. But this wouldn't be one of those.

'Aston asked the audit to keep checking, isolating the records of Parker's work, and started Kim cross-checking other departments for things like complaints about work not done, which departments had been involved in certain decisions and so on. You know the kind of thing.'

I didn't but I nodded my head as if I did.

'At that point he was the only one who had the whole picture. He had told the Leader roughly what he was doing.'

She meant Teddy McCormack. The leader of the majority group and the council leader were always one and the same person, and once the Leader had been elected the convention was to drop their name and use the title.

'He had that much sense,' she said, 'but I don't know if anyone else ever knew all of it. He was paranoiac about them finding out.'

'So why did he tell you?'

She grinned.

'You don't understand. By that time he had enough bits and pieces to set a formal investigation in motion. But even the Leader wouldn't agree to that without consulting a few key people. Look, it's like espionage. Suspicion can fall pretty rapidly on whoever's doing the investigation. If you fail you could have taken a cut to look the other way. If you succeed, your motives may be suspect. So you let as many people as possible know as soon as possible while keeping it as secret as possible. Something of that size. It needs to be a group decision.'

'But wait a minute,' I said. 'If they were digging around and reading records and asking questions, wouldn't these people suspect?'

'Not necessarily. I told you the internal audit is always poking around. There's always a good reason. Thievery, wastage. It's like bailing out a leaky boat.'

'So what did they find out?'

She sat back and sighed.

'That's the problem. Unravelling this sort of thing can take years. We know what was happening. Someone was feeding Parker's the information for their tenders, and the same person was making sure their specifications went through. We knew that the problem had to be in the quantity surveyors. Prove it though. That's something else.'

'Why was it so difficult if you knew that much?'

Sophie came back in with the coffee and Spid waited till she'd handed the cups round and settled herself.

'Lots of people had their fingerprints on all of these things, that's why. It's a team with up to ten people or more looking at everything. Okay. Let's say the person's quite high up. That cuts it down to three or four. Usually you'd set some kind of trap. Try and arrange for your person to be dealing with one project. But if you're wrong, you'll probably have alerted everyone, and then you'll never get any proof.'

'What about the money? The payoffs. The profits. The villains should at least have more money.'

'How can you tell? These guys aren't stupid. They don't nip round the corner to the building society. They put it in Swiss numbered accounts, or they take it in presents that are hard to trace. Free holidays, time share apartments, video equipment. You name it.'

'It sounds hopeless,' I said. 'How do you ever catch anyone at it?'

'Sometimes if they don't suspect anything the traps work. There's a procedure you can go into even when there's no hard evidence. If you can establish a circumstantial link, you can suspend them. They come in one morning and you've locked them out of their offices, taken charge of their files so they can't destroy the evidence, then you tell them they're suspended and warn them not to talk to any of their colleagues on pain of instant dismissal. Then everybody flogs themselves to death to make it stand up. That's what Aston was just about to do.'

'What?'

'He rang me in the afternoon, and said we'd have a meeting that evening, because he thought he had the person we wanted. He was going to get a statement that afternoon which would nail everything down.'

'Who was he going to suspend?'

'Not a bloody clue. We've all been racking our brains ever since.'

'Who else did he tell?'

'Oh. The Leader, me and two other chairs. We were at a group meeting and then we waited for him to turn up and when he didn't we went home.'

'Did any of you say anything to anyone?'

'Absolutely not. It's not something you gossip about. Not the people involved anyway.'

'Why didn't any of you think of telling all this to the police? I mean it sounds quite important to me.'

She looked uncomfortable.

'No one thinks there's a connection. I don't. The person wouldn't know. There's no way Aston would drop a hint that we were going to suspend him next morning. And besides.' She paused, thinking about what she was going to say. 'It wasn't a killing matter. Oh. People might have lost money. It would have been bad publicity. But things of this size the ringleaders hardly ever get prosecuted. It's so hard to prove. Sometimes the small fry end up in court but mostly the big ones just leave, and you stop it that way. Sometimes you can squeeze compensation out of the contractors, but it would have been a contest that they had a more than fifty-fifty chance of winning. The investigation might have got nowhere in the end. Something else might have come up. The members might change or retire. Too many possibilities.'

Marvellous. If that was true, it made nonsense of my big motive. But I wasn't entirely convinced.

'What about Walter? Don't you think he might have got on to something and been killed for it? It's like too much of a coincidence, don't you think?'

'Yes,' she said slowly. 'I think I'd better talk to the Leader about this tomorrow.'

'Tell him to talk to the police,' I said. 'That's what needs doing.'

She nodded her head, preoccupied.

'I'd better be going,' she said.

I said thank you sincerely, and I meant it.

Sophie saw her out and came back. She sat on the sofa and sprawled out with her head thrown back. She was a stranger, I thought, and I had no idea what she was thinking or feeling.

It was well past midnight and the moon had travelled several yards to the right of where it had been when we sat down to talk. That seemed a very long time ago. It had been a long day altogether, and now all I wanted to do was sleep. I was trying to consider what Spid had told me but my mind was a jumble of disconnected thoughts and impressions.

'I'm going to bed,' Sophie said abruptly.

Funny thing. A couple of hours earlier I'd been running up the stairs eager to talk to her.

'Do you think maybe we should talk about things?' I asked her.

'Not tonight. Maybe tomorrow.'

I was too tired to argue.

'The funeral's tomorrow,' I told her. 'Are you coming with me?'

'Are they cremating him? He ought to be cremated.'

'No,' I told her. 'He would have wanted to be buried. It's what we're used to.'

Suzanne would know that.

Are you coming anyway?'

'No.' she said. 'I can't take funerals, and I hardly knew him.'

I stood up. I felt sad and angry and racked by frustration.

'Don't come then,' I said loudly.

She didn't reply and without looking at her I stalked to the door, pulled it open, went through and slammed it shut behind me.

So much for good intentions.

Chapter 29

The council was arranging a big memorial service at the church in the High Street but the funeral was supposed to be a small quiet ceremony no flowers please and it very nearly was.

The cemetery was out of the way for a start. North of the borough. Up the old A10 in the direction of Cambridge, then turning off after the Great North Road. This was the sort of area I felt was never meant to be part of London. Neat new houses behind carefully tended hedges, bordering wide dual carriageway roads choked with traffic going somewhere. Interspersed with these were clean new postwar factory buildings, now converted to work on electronic components, and they'd never even smelled the dust, grime and smoke of the city. Facing the turn-off to the cemetery was a reservoir, slate-grey water still and hard as a mirror. It was a setting that made me shiver. Not a spot where I'd want to spend all eternity.

Coming on top of all that the cemetery itself seemed pleasant enough. The arch of the gateway led into a curving drive, lined with trees. Mostly English, small oaks and beeches, but on the curve there was a foreign invader, a huge, beautiful eucalyptus. The drive ended in a splashing semi-circle of gravel faced by a chapel which had the air of a miniature cathedral.

It wasn't a rural elegy, but when I looked away from the lounging photographers and the TV crew, out over the field of gravestones and small flowering trees, the morning had a feeling of peace and dignified calm.

Suzanne was already there, in black down to her ankles, Helen standing next to her, indomitable. Aston's sisters, just flown in from Canada where they lived, were lined up beside them at the door. They were both big, good-looking women, strikingly alike, with straightened hair, hatted and veiled. I had seen Gloria, the older one, a few years ago when she came to visit Aston, but the last time I'd spoken to Charmaine she'd been a toddler wearing a short singlet and a pair of flowered panties. We gazed at each other, the transformation filling us with the usual amazement.

'Oh my God,' she said. 'This is Sammy?'

I smiled at her. She reached out to grab me and hug me tight. Then she murmured that she would see me later at the house, and let me go.

Inside the building it was like a replay of the inquest. Borelli was there, looking thuggish in his black suit. He was flanked by two plain-clothes men who kept turning round to look at people. Shelagh and Marcie were sitting opposite them with Kevin in attendance. Near the back, three rows of seats were occupied by what seemed to be a solid mass of black people, but when I looked closely I could see there a few whites among them. These were from Aston's union. Mostly middle-aged women, and they sat together with an air of grim watchfulness, as if they'd come to see the brother right. Eva and Granny were sitting near them, Granny with a look of lively curiosity. She'd come to see the show and see it she would, to hell with what anybody thought.

I sat next to Spid and the council Leader, because we were going to carry him to the graveside together with some people from the union. It had seemed strange having a woman as a bearer but Suzie said Aston would have liked it, and I guessed she was right.

When the service started I hardly noticed. I was preoccupied with what I would say. Suzie had asked me to get up and talk during the service and I couldn't say no, although I was scared stiff of doing it badly, making a fool of myself and letting down Aston.

I'd been thinking about it all morning. I'd considered reading a poem, but he hadn't been a poetry man, and everything I could think of to say about his life sounded pompous or angry. He'd been kind and a mate, and the only things in which he was really interested were politics, sex and hanging out with people and goddam whoever killed him. But those weren't the right things to say and eventually the only thing that would stay in the front of my mind was a story I'd told my son when he was little. He'd liked it and a number of times afterwards he'd asked me to tell him that story again.

The memory was disturbing, because I'd wanted him to be there with me, but when I asked his mother she'd frowned, and said that funerals were depressing. She didn't think he should go. I hadn't argued. There were times when we were on a knife edge, but she had custody and I was in no position to antagonise her.

In any case I understood her attitude. In her experience funerals had been singular and upsetting occasions she was forced to attend. She found it impossible to believe that I remembered them as events of tremendous interest from which I'd come away with feelings that were sad but also warm and reassuring. Whenever a relative or a friend of the family died I'd be there, sedate among the mourners, taking in every detail of the show.

By the time I was about ten I'd been to several of these affairs, and while the deaths could be sad the funerals were mostly pleasurable and exciting. My son would never, I thought, know what it was to be part of such communal rituals. He had none of things I'd wanted for him. Sunk in my own thoughts I was shaking my head and clicking my tongue like an old man, and when someone nudged me I assumed it was Spid trying to shut me up, but she was merely telling me it was my turn.

I mounted the platform with the panic-stricken thought that it was too late to plan anything else, and saw Tommy right in front of me, with the old ladies I'd seen before on either side of him. He'd gone through another of his changes. In his new three-piece black suit with a gold chain across his belly, he looked like a patriarch, hewn out of rock, his eyes gleaming fiercely out of deep, shadowed sockets.

The sight steadied me, and without wavering I told the story about how I'd gone swimming with Aston in one of the sugar estate canals back home. For some reason we used to call the place Welly and we weren't supposed to be there, either because it was dangerous or it somehow damaged the cane, and halfway through the fun one of the sugar company's watchmen had swooped down, picked up my clothes and disappeared. We'd been about eleven then and we only wore shirts and short pants, no shoes and socks. Aston had grabbed his in time, and he gave me his shirt without prompting. I wrapped it round me and we walked home, both half naked, jeered at by the kids in the streets we passed through. I was silent and anguished, worrying about what my mother would say, but Aston, always bolder than me, had laughed and joked all the way.

'They say about some people,' I said, 'that they'd give you the shirt off their backs. Well, I know that he would do that for anyone in need, because he did.'

I sat down without looking at anyone. Just in case. Now I could start worrying about carrying the coffin.

In the event no one slipped or stumbled and we didn't drop it on the ground, the sort of disaster that would have given Granny a good laugh. I had thought it would be a difficult matter having Spid next to me, but it was oddly companionable, and our burden felt light and warm. It was drizzling a little, and I wondered how Aston would feel about lying here among these foreign trees. At home it was hibiscus flowers and mango trees.

Tommy used to say that he didn't want to leave his bones in this country and as we set the coffin down I glanced across at him to see if I could tell what he was thinking, but his eyes were far away and he didn't look back at me.

I was panting a little, although I couldn't believe that was merely from the weight I'd been carrying, and I felt slack and exhausted. So I stood there, ignoring the singing, and the praying and crying, and watched the trees and the birds flying around them until it was time to go home.

Chapter 30

When we got back it had only just gone lunchtime but there was a party atmosphere at Suzanne's place. I had a feeling that was because of all the black people there. Either by coincidence or because she'd planned it that way, there were about equal numbers of black and whites in the house. Looking round it struck me that this was an unusual sight. In a city where so many races lived together there'd never be more than a very few black people at a white social occasion, and if it was a black do there'd be even fewer whites present.

Aston's sisters were staying in the house and now they'd taken their hats off they looked at ease and excited, as if they'd had a good time and were just ready to murder a drink and a few sandwiches. It wasn't that they weren't grieving. They were. They just couldn't be mournful about it.

Tommy was in his element, sitting in the corner, clustered round by women. He was telling stories about Aston and quoting things he'd said, but listening to him I was sure that most of them were lies, and that he was making it all up on the spur of the moment.

Teddy McCormack, the council Leader, cornered me as I was going over to the old man. He was trying to look suitably gloomy, but he was a gregarious person and his eyes were shining with the effect of the drink and the company. He took my elbow and led me to a quiet spot near the door.

'I had a talk with Spid,' he murmured. 'I think you ought to know that I'm going to consult a few people this afternoon and I'll get in touch with the police after that. Probably tomorrow morning.'

I told him I was glad about that and that I hoped things would work out, and I was just going to ask him a few questions about the swindle and the investigation when Suzie came up and pulled me away.

'Come on, Sammy. Something I want to show you.'

We went upstairs to their big bedroom. The bed was covered in clothes, a couple of suitcases and various objects, as if she didn't sleep there any more. They were mostly Aston's belongings and I had the feeling that somehow he was there, lying hidden amongst them. She'd been giving these things away over the last few days, almost feverishly, as if she wanted to get rid of everything that reminded her. Now I had a good look at her I thought her face seemed haggard and lined. In a few days she had aged considerably.

'Hey listen, kid,' I said. 'You really ought to keep some of these things.'

She looked at the bed.

'There's plenty more,' she said. 'Besides, what am I to do with them? I don't have a chick or a child.'

That was the phrase we'd used at home for someone with no responsibilities. Not a chick or a child. Aston must have taught it to her.

She went to the wardrobe and pulled out a jacket. She held it out to me.

'It's nearly new. I don't want anyone else to have it. I bought it for his birthday. And take anything else you want.'

Suddenly she pulled it back, felt inside and took out a pocket computer.

'I was looking for this,' she said. 'They came and took his desk diary, but I couldn't find this one.'

She weighed it in her hand, considering.

'It doesn't matter anyway. He used to transfer everything

important to the desk diary. And he didn't put much in here. Just things that happened on the run. He used to think something might go wrong and wipe out all the information. Why don't you take it, Sammy? Take it.'

I took it and pulled it open.

'So it wouldn't have any stuff in it about what he was doing?'

She shook her head.

'I don't think so. Even if it did it would be protected by the password. He said it was the safest kind of password, a word that was private and only meant something to him. He used to say that was the lesson of Rumpelstiltskin, the guy really understood the idea of codes and unless a real fairy godmother came along it would be safe.'

She was beginning to reproduce Aston's patterns of speech, but she was talking too fast, too brightly and I knew that in a minute the tears would fall.

'He thought you might be able to figure it out, Sam, but he said that he had no intention of letting a bum like you get his hands on his private and personal diaries.'

I'd been right and she started crying halfway through the sentence. I put my arms round her and patted her gently on the back. Aston. I felt a stab of resentment. I was tired, worn out, wading through this world of tears, all for him.

Charmaine came to the door, and paused when she saw us like that. Then I raised my eyebrows at her and she came in and put her arm round Suzie too.

'Suzie,' she whispered. 'The mayor's leaving. I'll tell him you're lying down.'

Suzanne pulled away immediately and began to dry her eyes.

'No,' she said. 'I'm coming.'

She squeezed my hand and went out, her arm round Charmaine. Left to myself I loosened my collar, dried off my neck and went to look in the mirror. I had a pleasant enough face, regular features, not too clapped out, and I was alive. All that was good, but I wondered if and when I'd stop envying Aston. 'That's morbid,' I muttered, suddenly aware of the reflection of myself standing there in his bedroom, among his belongings, my mind in turmoil. I swung round and at the same time the computer fell off the bed where I'd left it. I picked it up and found myself looking at it again.

It was strange that he'd left it in that jacket, and that Suzanne hadn't discovered it till then. Perhaps not so strange because it would probably have found its way to me one way or the other. But he'd also told her that I was the only one who might be able to figure out the password.

Tell all that to my granny or my mum and they'd have been certain about what it was. 'He's trying to tell you something,' they'd say firmly.

I laughed a little at the idea, but the fact was that it had come into my head because I'd grown up listening to stuff like that, and somewhere inside I could never be entirely sure that the old folks, against all reason, were not sometimes right.

I pressed the keys and looked at the blank screen. Then I keyed in the name of our village. Five letters. Just right. Nothing. I looked at it for a while. I couldn't think. Then I got it, and I keyed in the word Welly, and the screen came alive. I nearly dropped the thing. I was trembling and I leaned against the wall for support. But after a while I got back in control and the party noises came back and I pulled myself together and scrolled through to the date Aston had died. There was only one entry, and to my disappointment it was a name I didn't recognise. Jen Miller. 3.30 p.m. On the next line there was a phone number.

I closed the door and picked up the extension next to the bed. I dialled the number and after a few rings a woman answered. She had a harsh high voice. Not young.

I told her who I was and I said I wanted to talk to her about her meeting with Councillor Edwards last week.

'I don't want to be involved,' she said immediately.

Undertones of the North. But she'd been living here in London for a long time.

'Mrs Miller,' I said. 'You are involved.'

I was too wound up to beat around the bush. I told her I could probably keep her name out of it if she let me know what they'd talked about, but if she didn't I could guarantee that the police would be round her house before the end of the day, followed shortly after by a bunch of photographers and reporters. That got through to her, as I'd expected, and she gave me her address and told me to come round.

I picked up the jacket and the computer, and went downstairs to say goodbye to Suzie. She was standing in the corridor talking to the council Leader, who was holding her hand and looking sincere. I guessed that the mayor had gone.

'Suzie,' I said without preliminaries. No time. 'Who's Jen Miller?'

She frowned.

'Jen Miller? The name's familiar, but I don't know.'

'Jen?' the Leader said. 'Jenny Miller? She's married to someone in the quantity surveyor's office. Richard. Richard Miller.'

Chapter 31

The house was on the fringe of the residential district where Aston and the Parkers lived, but it was in a side street off the part of the main road that constituted the local shopping centre. The shops were pretty posh, as befitted the area: patisseries, bookshops and a couple of bistros, but the DIY centre was on the corner of the Millers' road, and as I turned down it I went past a yard full of timber and sheets of metal.

Jenny Miller must have been looking out for me, because she opened the door in practically the same moment that I rang the bell.

She had dull straggly brown hair, but everything else about her was sharp and tight, from her light blue eyes down to her taut wiry calves, and she gave me the impression of quivering slightly all the time. A nervous jangling woman I guessed to be in her mid-forties and not easy about it.

She let me in willingly enough. The house was one of the older ones, with an attic and a cellar, and they'd knocked through the ground floor, so that it was all one big room, with a staircase leading up to the floor above, then reversing its direction and going on up to the floor above that. The whole effect was elegant and stylish as if they'd spent a lot of money on getting it right. This house would fetch a price well above the market for the area. But the woman in front of me in her baggy brown skirt and sweater had no style at all, and she didn't look as if she belonged in that place.

'Who are you exactly?' she said.

'I'm continuing the investigation that Councillor Edwards was engaged in. Sampson Dean,' I said.

I was, after all, wearing a pretty nice black suit, and after the morning's work I didn't have to struggle to look stern and official. She was convinced, all right. But she was still worried.

'I don't know,' she said. 'I rang Councillor Edwards because I had to talk to someone, and I'd met him before a few times. He was such a nice man. I voted for him, you know.'

I nodded sympathetically, but with reserve. I was trying for that weird blend of sycophancy and authority I'd seen the undertaker radiating, and I ushered her into the nearest armchair, then sat down opposite her and leaned forward.

'We simply need to clear up a few details. We know that the councillor came to see you, but we need to know how much you told him.'

'I don't want to get involved,' she said again.

'Don't worry,' I said. 'We don't think that it has any bearing, but we've got to clear the matter up, don't we? Is Richard in, by the way?'

'No,' she said sharply. 'He doesn't come here any more. That's why I rang up. About the money really.'

'Yes.'

Now that she'd started she took it from the top, and her story had a neatness and cohesion which told me it had already been shaped and rehearsed by Aston's questions and the things he was interested in. She told me that they hadn't ever been as prosperous as the house suggested. Richard had got a lot of discounts for the work that had been done here, and it cost practically nothing. That was because of his job, but he'd told her not to talk about it because there was so much jealousy and spite over these things. You had to be careful.

The next thing was that he'd started to take on private work, some of it abroad. He'd taken her and the children on holiday more than once in the year, a friend in the trade had lent them villas, oh, in lots of places, the South of France, Spain, Morocco. They'd been all over. But, of course, he'd had to go away by himself. On these occasions she'd noticed that he was carrying a lot of money, and he'd said that he had to pay foreign contractors. But by then she was smarter than that. She'd looked through his things and found letters from Switzerland. From a bank.

'I wasn't looking for anything,' she said hastily. 'I just found them.'

At that point she looked straight at me. That was the clue. When she thought she was being dishonest she looked me in the eyes. The rest of the time her gaze skittered vaguely and restlessly around the walls, the carpet, the ceiling. Anywhere.

She'd confronted him then. Sort of. And he'd told her that he was doing private work, and being paid in cash. He had to keep it quiet because the stupid bureaucrats down the town hall might say he was breaking the rules.

She sounded bitter about that, and I wondered whether she was angry at her husband or at the town hall bureaucrats who were trying to stop him picking up all that lovely money. I must have let something show on my face and she misinterpreted it.

'Sorry,' she muttered.

I shrugged.

'Oh. We all hate bureaucracy. And I must admit the civic centre's full of it.'

That reassured her and she went on. What really worried her was the fact that she was by now beginning to suspect that Richard had another woman. Women could sense these things. He was out all hours, and he was moody and irritable. Paid no attention to her or the children. She had ignored it and kept her fingers crossed. Hoped it would come to an end. But it had got worse in the last year or so and he had capped it all a couple of months ago by going off with a girl young enough to be his granddaughter, who worked as a secretary in the department.

Ah hah.

She misinterpreted my look again.

'Oh. I don't care any more,' she said. She gave a little laugh.

A nasty sound. 'I wish them joy of each other. It's just that I cannot manage.'

I tried to look as if I believed that bit while she told me the rest. She had let her secretarial skills go, all this time married to Richard. And in any case jobs were impossible to get for mature women even when you could do the work standing on your head. They all wanted cute young things in high heels. She worked part time in the nursery but the money was useless. And the pittance that Richard proposed to give her was nothing when you considered all the money he'd made while they were together. When she'd spoken to him about it he'd simply denied everything. He said she'd misunderstood about the private work and the money, and all he really had was his salary. Barefaced cheek. That was what she couldn't stand.

That was when she'd got in touch with Councillor Edwards. She knew that Richard was afraid of him. He was a dangerous snooper, Richard said. Conceited, jumped up, arrogant. She stopped, and I realised that I had been bracing myself for the black bastard bit of the sentence.

'Sorry,' she said again. 'I'm not like that. If a man can do the job. He was a good councillor.'

'Yes, of course,' I said encouragingly. 'Don't worry. Go on.'

But I'd heard the gist of it. The rest was a reprise of Richard's domestic crimes and her financial woes. She had been a doormat for twenty years, she said, and she wasn't going to take it any more.

Listening to her, it struck me that this woman's rage would haunt her husband, probably for the rest of his life. In a couple of years the pain would have receded, and with any luck she would find another man very like Richard, who would treat her in more or less the same way. But she'd always hate the first one.

We'd been talking for well over an hour and round about half past four we heard a key grating in the door outside.

'That will be my daughter,' she said. A signal for me to go.

'By the way,' I asked her. 'Did Richard know about Councillor Edwards' visit?'

She compressed her lips and shook her head tightly.

'No. Of course not.'

I stood up then, thanked her, said goodbye and promised that we would be in touch. In the hallway on the way out I passed the daughter. She gave me a curious look and I smiled and said good afternoon.

It may have been the effect of a long day at school, but she already had a sullen disappointed cast to her features. Her father and the girl young enough to be his granddaughter flashed through my mind. I had no idea whether the man would think it was worth it, but I guessed that if these women had anything to do with the matter Richard would have an awful lot for which to answer.

Chapter 32

I went home, took off the black suit and rang Aubrey. I had considered going to see Borelli, but although I felt I was now beginning to get a grip on what had happened, I knew he would think that all this was simply more rumours, guesses, hints. It might be different after the council Leader had been to see him, but I couldn't tell. With a dragnet out for Dalton, and an established public focus on the estate, it would take a lot to make him change course and point the investigation towards another quadrant. I had to have more.

There was something else. Aston was my childhood friend, my homeboy. What had been done to him was done to me. To Borelli it was a case. For that reason alone I didn't trust him.

I told Aubrey we had a target. Now we were walking in Aston's footsteps, and I arranged to pick him up later.

Next I looked up Spid in the phone book. I owed her this one. No answer. I guessed she was at the civic centre having a meeting. The Leader would be there too. I'd just have to catch them later.

Out the window I saw Chummy putting a sports bag in the Porsche. He was wearing 501s, Nikes and a striped shirt. After a hard working week surrounded by long-legged young women, and trapped in designer suits and wine bars, he was going home to relax and refresh the batteries. He looked round and waved at me. I waved back, thinking about Miller.

If I was reading Jenny's story right Richard Miller had finally achieved a similar kind of lifestyle, thirty years after young Chummy. Perhaps he would kill to preserve it. But I didn't think so. If what I'd been told by everyone involved was correct he didn't have to. Maybe he'd panicked, but I didn't think it would make a difference. Aston wasn't soft, and there was no way, I thought, that he would let himself be killed by a panicky quantity surveyor who'd been married to a woman like Jenny.

This was sheer nonsense, because I knew anything could happen, but that was how I felt.

In any case, there had to be other people involved in the scam, a chain of evidence connecting Miller to the Parkers, which a bit of digging would uncover. Otherwise Aston wouldn't have bothered about suspending him immediately. Miller was only one link in the chain and when I knew who the others were and what they knew I would have an idea about whether they'd had a strong enough motive for murder. My going to see him might tip them off so that they had time to start destroying the evidence of their swindle. But that wasn't my problem. I would ring Spid immediately after I saw Miller, and in any case, if I alarmed them sufficiently they might do something to give themselves away.

Aubrey was at the usual place, outside the nick in Harrow Road. Tonight was Friday night. Maman would be cooking black pudding or another of her famous dishes and the house would be full of people. I hadn't wanted to go there, not with my mind full of turmoil and haunted by memory.

'How was the funeral?' Aubrey asked.

I said it had been good, the mayor had been there with a lot of big shots, but also old friends, relatives and some people from the union. He nodded, satisfied.

I told him more about Miller and what I wanted from him.

'How are you going to do it then?'

I glanced over at him. It was techniques and concrete processes which stirred his interest, not the speculation about motives and purposes.

I told him Jenny Miller had given me a clue when she'd talked about her husband's reaction to Aston. Parker's attitude was similar but he was also in love with physical violence. He would be at home on the football terraces with the Inner City Firm. Give those guys a Stanley knife and they'd be at your throat like a hungry Rottweiler. Just say kill. A middle-class tosser like Miller was different. The stronger his racial feelings were the more likely he was to be scared stiff that a black man would jump out round the next corner and say boo. He would find our presence alone nerve-racking and threatening. One black man would be an awkward enough proposition, but standing next to two or three blacks made some white people react as if they were surrounded by the entire Zulu army. If that was the way he was, and if he didn't go for reasonable argument, we'd just have to lean on him.

Aubrey chuckled. He looked teasingly at me.

'A respectable gentleman like you,' he said. 'You taking this thing serious.'

The address Jenny had given me was a private block on the main street near the art college. There was a drive and a car park, both guarded by an iron barrier secured by a big padlock, so we parked in the street. It was about eight, but there didn't seem to be many people about and we went on up the carpeted wooden stairs without meeting anyone. There was a thick red carpet along the corridor and it was lit by discreet spotlights sunk into the ceiling. On the way Aubrey stopped to look at a big reproduction of an abstract painting on the wall. That's the kind of place it was.

Miller opened the door with a self-important scowl on his face, as if he was wondering who on earth had the nerve to ring his doorbell unannounced.

'What do you want?'

Rude, but I was accustomed to that. The only reason I noticed was that I was concentrating hard on his every move, trying to figure out what sort of animal he was.

'I want to talk to you, Mr Miller.'

He was a short, stocky, red-faced man, over fifty, with sandy hair going in the middle, and pale protruding blue eyes. When he heard this, he glared up at us, his eyes opening wide and standing further out.

'To me?' He looked contemptuous. 'Who are you anyway?'

I told him who I was and that I was looking into certain matters that Aston had been investigating.

'I've nothing to say to you,' he said abruptly. He fidgeted with the door, but I was leaning on it so that it couldn't be closed without warning.

'I've just come from your wife's house,' I said. 'She told me a lot. You want to talk about it out here?'

I could have sworn that I saw a leap of fright flash across behind his stare. He dithered for a moment and in the middle of the pause a young woman appeared behind him and called out.

'Who is it, love?'

He turned round without moving from in front of the entrance.

'People from work.'

'Well don't stand at the door. Let them in.'

He looked angry and flustered, but I gave him the kind of smile which told him that I wasn't going away, and eventually he stood back and let us come in.

She stood in the middle of the big split-level room, smiling as if she was going to recognise us, and when she didn't her smile grew a little uncertain. But she was determined to play hostess. She wasn't young enough to be his granddaughter but she was in her twenties and luscious enough to give the average grandad more than a few palpitations. She had tight permed brown hair with blonde streaks, and she was wearing short shorts with high heeled sandals. Above that was a halter top which exposed her back and dramatised her breasts.

'Hello,' she said, coming forward to shake hands. 'I'm Sandy. Which department do you work in?'

Her voice had a polite North London sound, and she seemed like a nice girl working at being a good companion. I told her our names and said that we didn't normally work at the civic centre. Miller had strutted past and sat down, ignoring the civilities, and she looked at him as if she couldn't understand his manners.

'Sit down,' she said. 'Would you like a drink?'

'Oh yes. Anything you've got.'

'Juice please,' Aubrey said.

She went over to the bar in the corner and we sat silently until she'd brought the drinks. She handed them round solicitously, showing off a lot of nice flesh as she did so, and Miller watched her with an expression that grew more and more sour by the minute.

'Confidential business I'm afraid, pet,' he said at last, and she raised her eyebrows, made a face, tossed her head, gave us a smile which said we must humour him, and left the room.

'I don't know what my wife said to you,' Miller said, 'but anything that frustrated cow tells you is liable to be all lies.'

To judge by his voice he was from up North too, like Jenny. They'd probably started out together in some place like Preston.

I told him what she'd said to me. By the time I'd finished the recital I was keyed up, pushed by an angry exaltation that I could feel pulsing in my temples, and I wasn't going to play any more games with him.

'I want to know,' I said, 'who's in it with you. I know it all benefits Parker & Son, but I don't know how you're connected, and who else in your department has a reason for keeping it quiet.'

He leaned forward and put his glass down on the white marble coffee table.

'I think we've just finished this conversation,' he said. 'You'd better go now.'

A door opened somewhere and Sandy came in hesitantly.

'Everything all right?'

She had to be listening, and the thought seemed to upset Miller.

'Yes,' he said angrily. 'Just go on. Get out. Go on.'

She disappeared. But her intervention seemed to have helped Miller get up a head of steam.

'I don't know what you're up to, but none of this is anything to do with Aston Edwards. He was killed by some yobbo up the youth centre. That's obvious. They arrested him. As for all this rubbish — even if it was true, why the hell would anyone want to kill him? There's a lot easier ways.'

There was no doubting his sincerity and for the first time since early that afternoon my heart sank. If that was true I had to be on the wrong track. He stood up.

'You go back and tell your bloody Leader that he can find out everything about it, except how to prove that something was going on. I'm packing it in, getting shot of the bloody civic centre and the whole borough, so the bloody lot of you can sod off. Go on, get out my house.'

Aubrey coughed, and I got up and hit Miller in the nose with a left, a quick pop, the kind of jab we used to use so as to discourage them from coming forward. I hit him with as much force as I could but it was a punch that was about speed and precision, shooting straight out from the shoulder through a straightening elbow, and it hurt rather than disabled people. The point was to surprise and disorientate him. Soften him up.

It worked exactly as ordered. Miller sat down abruptly and put his hands to his face. His eyes were glazed and shocked, rolling around in his head. In a moment the blood began trickling through his fingers.

There was a scream and Sandy came flying in. She ran to his side and began prying his fingers apart.

'Richard,' she wailed. 'Richard. Are you all right, Richard?'

He muttered something incoherent, and she ran out and came back almost immediately with a wet towel. She tipped his head back and began dabbing at his face.

'Don't tip his head back like that,' I told her. 'It builds up the pressure and makes it worse. Just hold his head straight and pinch his nostrils together. He'll be all right.'

'You bastard,' she screeched at me. 'You bastard. Get out. I'm ringing the police right now.'

She had Richard's head cradled against her breasts and she didn't move, but I guessed she'd try for the phone in a moment.

'Okay,' I said. I turned to Aubrey who hadn't moved throughout all this. 'Bring us that telephone.'

It was the cordless sort. He got up, picked it up and brought it over, looking at it curiously. I held it up in front of Richard's eyes.

'Richard,' I said. 'Sandy's going to call the cops.'

It got through and he shook his head, then took the towel away from his face.

'No,' he said. 'Don't do that.'

'He's all right now,' I told Sandy. 'We'll just talk a minute and get this straightened out.'

'What is going on, Richard?' she demanded. 'Why don't you ring the police? What do they want?'

'Never mind,' he said. 'Just leave us alone for a bit. There's a good girl.'

'No,' she said. 'Richard, I want to know what's going on.'

He sat up with a jerk that nearly spilled her on to the floor.

'Shut up,' he shouted. 'Shut up you silly cow and do what you're told.'

She stared at him for a moment, then got up and walked off into the next room, slamming the door behind her. I went after her and opened it. She was lying on a pink satin bed with her face in the crook of her elbow.

'Sandy,' I said. 'Look at me.'

She looked round, her eyes brimming with tears.

'Don't worry, love,' I said. 'We won't hurt him. Just talk to him a bit. Just stay where you are. Okay?'

She nodded and turned away again. I closed the door and went back.

I sat on the arm of Richard's chair and turned his chin round to look up at me.

'You know something, Richard, treat her like that and in a year or so she's going to screw you up much worse than you think Jenny's going to.'

'What do you want?' he said. 'I told you. It's nothing to do with Aston. It isn't.'

I put my hands round his neck. He didn't move or try to hit

me, although one of his hands came up and made ineffectual pawing motions at mine.

'Listen, dickhead,' I said. I didn't have to pretend to the rage I could feel throbbing in my voice. 'Let me be the judge of that. That guy was my best friend. We grew up together and I'll do anything. Anything. You understand me. Anything. The next thing I want to hear out your mouth is names.'

He started talking then. It was as if the punch had knocked all the stuffing out of him, and I guessed also that he was in shock. He was probably a terror with Swiss bankers but subjecting him to a moment of sudden violence had turned his world upside down. Maybe it had also occurred to him that if there was no evidence it didn't matter what he said. Come to think of it I'd have hated to drag him into court so that he could sit in the witness box and tell the story of how two black men burst into his flat and beat a confession out of him. All in all I suspected that he was pretty safe, and after what had happened, talking was a much healthier option than keeping quiet.

There were three of them in the office. He was the most senior, second from the top. The rest were juniors. They didn't know all that much about what was going on, but they did what he wanted. There was an architect who did things from time to time, and other people he would run across when it was necessary. None of the names meant anything to me.

'Who told you what they wanted and paid you off? Parker?'

He shook his head. No. He never spoke to Parker except in the way of normal business. It was Marcie who co-ordinated everything.

'What? Marcie Connor?'

He smiled at me contemptuously.

'That's right. Good old Marcie. She put it all together.'

Marcie had recruited him, he said. They'd gone away to a training conference and they'd had a good time. She was unbelievable. The following week she had asked him to make sure that the specifications on one of Parker's jobs went through. This was nearly four years ago and at the time he'd been in a different position. He was worried about her telling Jenny. With

Marcie you never knew. I could believe that, but it was the sort of self-justification a man like Miller would always offer. The woman tempted me.

The rest was plain sailing. Things had got difficult over the last six months or so, after Aston had started sniffing around, and they'd begun to play it by the book, in case the internal audit turned up anything they'd overlooked. He swore it had nothing to do with Aston's death. After all, Richard hadn't fallen for any accounting traps. And as for Marcie, if anyone was stupid enough to offer details which implicated her she could tough it out. They'd left no tracks.

Besides, once the investigation proper started, there were all kinds of options. He had seen these things fall apart more than once when they tried to bring it to court. The right politicians could bring all kinds of pressures to bear on the right people. In the nature of things it could take years to unravel, and Aston himself had been in a hurry because if he'd been selected he was on the way out, and everything would go on hold during the election period. This was something he could start, but there was no way he could finish it, and everyone knew that. It would have taken a totally crazy person to try and kill him over this.

Talking about it seemed to bring him back to himself and at the end he gave me the old pop-eyed stare.

'I'll deny all this you know. You can't just beat confessions out of people. You won't have a leg to stand on.'

He was right, but now the cat was out of the bag, I intended to give the council a shot at getting him. I picked up the phone and rang Spid. She answered on the third ring.

'Hang on a mo,' she said. 'I've just come in.'

I hung on.

'Can I go to the loo?' Miller said, and I gave him permission with a gesture.

'Watch him,' I told Aubrey.

Spid came back and I told her I was at Miller's place and what he'd said. I told her too, about Jenny Miller and her meeting with Aston. After her initial surprise she was pretty businesslike, listening carefully and only asking the sort of questions which would let her get things straight.

Halfway through this account Miller came back and sat down like a good little boy. I couldn't tell what he was thinking because his eyes had clouded over and his expression was dull and impassive.

I ended by telling her that she ought to make sure tonight that the office was secure, in case anyone tried to destroy evidence.

'I know what to do,' she said, sounding a little impatient.

'Have you talked to the police?'

'Not yet.' There was a pause in which I could hear her breathing. 'Look, I wouldn't bank on too much on this lot,' she said. 'The good news is that this tells us a lot more than we knew before. We know who to concentrate on. The bad news is that we're not a lot nearer to making a credible case. In some ways you've made things worse.'

I'd had a suspicion that was how things stood, but listening to her say it didn't make me feel any better.

Chapter 33

I asked Aubrey to come back home with me. I didn't want to go to Maman's house and I couldn't think of anywhere else to go, but I didn't want to go there alone.

The pubs were just letting people out, and we kept going past little groups of people crossing the road to their cars. Once a man ran across in front of me, forcing me to brake. It was obvious, I thought, that he didn't know what a blundering fool I was, or he'd never have taken that chance with his life.

Going through Camden Town I put it straight to Aubrey.
'Do you think they killed him?'
'Who?'
'That town hall bunch. Marcie. Parker.'
He was silent for a moment.
'They're not wallies.'
The house was dark. No Chummy. I parked in his usual space with a flourish, and Aubrey grinned at me. The evening didn't seem to have lowered his spirits the way it had mine, and I avoided looking back at him.

On the way up the stairs I could hear the phone ringing and I ran for it with the conviction that it would stop before I got there. But it didn't.
'Marcie.'
'Marcie? This is a surprise.'

'I bet it is,' she said. 'I hear you've been busy. Trying to stitch me up.'

'Did you have something to tell me?'

'It won't work, you know. You know we were all at a reception when Aston was killed. And the other thing. You're in real trouble. I've advised Richard Miller to go to the police. They'll probably nick you tomorrow.'

Not good news.

'Maybe I can help you,' she said. 'As a matter of fact you've probably made things easier for us. What you've done: it's your word against Richard's. It's only your word that he said anything. The best thing would be for everyone to calm down and drop the whole matter.'

I was busy trying to work out where this was going and I didn't reply.

'What do you say? Why don't we meet and try to sort this out?'

She sounded so reasonable.

'Okay.'

'Tonight? Let's make it as soon as poss.'

'Okay.'

'I'll meet you at midnight on the building site. Where we were before. Remember it?'

'Yes. Why there? What about the security? Dogs and that.'

She laughed.

'They come every couple of hours and we'll be gone long before their next tour. Don't worry. Besides. No one will see us there and it's a nice place. Didn't you like it?'

'Okay.'

'See you later.'

I stood there listening to the dialling tone, trying to get my mind round what she'd said. Aubrey, coming in from the kitchen with his glass of orange squash, looked at me curiously, and I told him.

'You're going?'

'Yes.'

'You're mad.'

'Why? I thought you didn't think it was them.'
He shrugged and gestured with the glass.
'You never know.'

The site was wrapped in deep shadows, brooded over by a giant crane, a watchful monster guarding the sleeping yard. The gate was unlocked and from there we could see the show house, the ground floor all lit up now, with the white electric glare of naked bulbs.

On the way I had told Aubrey that Marcie might try to bribe me, which might tell me more about how she had worked the business down at the civic centre. It might even have something to do with Aston, although I didn't really think that any more. But the truth was that I was curious and there didn't seem to be any other options to pursue. I wanted to hear what she had to say.

'Snoop around,' I told Aubrey, 'and make sure there's nobody else here. If you see a bunch of navvies with iron bars run like buggery.'

He slipped inside the gate and I waited. I wasn't too worried about Miller's complaint, if he did go to the police. A quick punch wasn't much and I could muddy the waters sufficiently to get away with it. What depressed me was the thought that Aston's enquiry hadn't been a real motive for his death. If that was so, then it probably was a random killing that might never be solved. Even worse was the thought that Borelli was right, and it might be something to do with Tony after all.

Aubrey came back.

'No one there except them.'

He pointed at the show house.

'Them?'

'Marcie, Parker and her husband.'

I'd thought she was coming alone but this was logical. On the other hand, that made three of them. I thought about it. Frank was a drunk, and I could handle Parker. Besides, Aubrey was with me. No problem.

The door of the house was propped open, throwing a square

of light out into the yard. I went past it and looked through the front window. The three of them were there. Parker leaned against the wall near the back, Marcie was pacing up and down, and Frank was sitting on the floor in one corner. They looked dressed up as if they'd been out somewhere. The men were wearing dark suits and Marcie was in a tight shiny black dress which hugged her body. As I watched Frank picked up the bottle which was standing on the floor next to him and took a long swig. Marcie gave him an impatient look and he took it away from his lips, wiped it with the palm of his hand and offered it to Parker who shook his head.

I rapped on the glass and Marcie looked round, saw me and came out into the hallway. I talked to her from outside the door.

'I thought we were going to be alone.'

'Not tonight,' she said. 'Come in.' She paused, catching sight of Aubrey for the first time. 'You're not alone either. Tell your friend to wait. Outside.'

'That makes three to one,' I said.

She clicked her tongue impatiently.

'All right. I'll tell Frank to wait outside with him. Okay?'

She turned round, called out, and Frank walked into the passage.

'Wait outside with him, Frank,' Marcie told him, and he came out, his eyes narrowed, looking around suspiciously. He stumbled a little as he came out and I gripped his elbow and helped him upright. His whisky breath was ferocious, coming at me in one savage burst, like an animal leaping from its cage. I shook my head, held my breath and went in after Marcie.

Parker was standing away from the wall and when I came in he stared at me without moving. I couldn't work out what mood he was in, but just to be on the safe side — my mum used to say it never hurt — I smiled at him and said good evening.

Actually I was smiling because in that moment I remembered slapping him in the chops. The only bright spot so far to the whole affair.

He gave me a tight little nod, and Marcie grinned, looking from one to the other of us.

'Come on boys,' she said. 'I know you've had your problems but let's kiss and make up.'

'Just tell him,' Parker said.

He seemed sober and in control of himself tonight.

Marcie shrugged.

'The first thing is what you're all het up about. I know what you said to Richard Miller and I swear to you that neither of us had anything to do with what happened to Aston. We were miles away, and it isn't something we would do. Keith flies off the handle, and he'd probably bash your face in if he got the chance, but he wouldn't kill you. And with Aston it just doesn't make sense. Not for us. I swear.'

I looked at Parker and he looked straight back at me. I could have huffed and puffed about it, but I believed her.

'I believe you,' I said.

'All right,' she said. 'It's just that we've had enough of you trying to fit us up.'

'I said I believed you.'

'Okay. You knocked Miller about tonight and he said the first thing that came into his head. It won't stand up in court or anywhere else and he'll say he was telling you what you wanted to hear because you beat him up. You with me so far?'

She seemed amused, even pleased by the situation, and her manner was teasing and provocative.

'But it might cause us a little trouble. Especially me, and I don't like that. It would help if you didn't remember what he said to you. And he could forget what you did to him. Fair offer?'

'No,' I said. 'It may be a fair offer to a man with a Swiss bank account. To me it's bollocks.'

Parker made an impatient sound, and she held her hand up to shush him. She moved closer to me.

'All right,' she said. 'Tell me what you want.'

Parker rumbled again, and she glanced round and frowned. Then she moved closer and stood in front of me with her hands on her hips and her legs spread so that they strained against the cloth of her skirt. She switched her hips, a tiny held-in movement, and there was a little excited smile on her face. In spite of all I knew about her I thought she looked good. In this mood she could probably twist half the civic centre round her little finger. I caught sight of Parker over her shoulder, and he was watching her with a sort of angry resignation. When my eyes met hers again she laughed a little, as if she knew what I'd been thinking.

'What is it?' she said. 'You could do with a car, instead of that heap of junk you're driving. Go on. Give us a clue.'

I had no idea what I was going to say, because at that point we heard footsteps on the wooden floor of the passageway, and Aubrey appeared at the door. The sight of him pulled Parker's hair trigger.

'What's he doing?' he said angrily.

I raised my eyebrows at Aubrey, but he kept coming, and as he moved a couple of paces into the room, I realised that Frank was behind him. In the same moment I saw Frank was also carrying a shotgun.

'Go over and stand against that wall,' he said.

Aubrey shrugged and kept on walking.

'Sorry,' he said as he passed me. 'I never saw the gun.'

'You too,' Frank said to me. He gestured and I walked backwards to stand beside Aubrey, keeping an eye on him.

Marcie laughed.

'Frank, what do you think you're doing?'

'I'm dealing with these two idiots. That's what I'm doing,' he said. 'You two get in the car and shove off. Leave this to me.'

Marcie laughed again.

'Look, Frank. Don't worry. They're not doing anything to us. We're okay. Just put the gun down and wait.'

'Don't tell me,' Frank said. 'I know what I'm doing.'

I watched him for an indication of how drunk he was, but it was hard to tell. One minute his speech would be slurred, the next he'd be speaking clearly. On the other hand, he was standing straight in the doorway, holding the gun steady, and he didn't seem anything like the stumbling drunk I'd taken him for only a little while ago.

'First the other one, now him.' He pointed the gun at me. 'There's only one way to deal with these dirty fuckers.'

This looked serious. Up to that point I'd felt like laughing along with Marcie but Frank's vague and watery blue eyes had suddenly focused and taken on a fixed stare that gave me the jitters. I couldn't tell whether it was the look on his face or the realisation that it had been Frank all along, but my left leg began trembling uncontrollably. I ignored it.

'The other one,' I said. 'You mean Aston. How did you deal with him?'

'He didn't,' Marcie said quickly. 'He's drunk, and shooting his mouth off. Leave him alone.'

'He's the one with the gun,' I said.

'I don't know why you're doing this, Frank,' she said, 'but it's pointless. Just give me the gun.'

'Shut up,' Frank said. 'Shut your fucking mouth, woman.'

Marcie shut it. It was the first time I'd ever seen her uncertain, and now I really began to be frightened.

'Frank,' Parker said in a kind of cajoling tone. 'Frank.'

'You too,' Frank said. 'Shut up. It takes a fucking man. A man. Your dad would have pissed on these. Pissed on them.'

I registered the phrase and at the back of my mind I wished he would use another one, but I had more pressing things to worry about. Keep him talking.

'Frank. Why Aston? Why?'

'Frank. Don't say any more,' Marcie said sharp and loud. 'You're drunk.'

'Course I'm drunk,' he said. 'I'm always fucking drunk.'

He laughed and I saw that he was drooling. His eyes wavered and he wiped his mouth unsteadily with the back of his hand. Aubrey moved but the gun came up and pointed like a snake striking.

'I've got business with them,' Frank said clearly. 'If you don't like it piss off out of it.'

'Frank,' I said. 'I asked you a question. Why Aston?'

'Frank,' Marcie said. Her voice had taken on a wailing tone. 'Tell him, Keith.'

Parker stepped forward and Frank moved back a pace waving the gun in a little arc of warning.

'Tch,tch,tch,tch,' he said. 'The man deserves an answer.' He was drooling from the corner of his mouth again. 'Councillor bloody Edwards was a trouble maker. It was my business too. He forgot that. They all think poor old Frank. Lives off Keith. The business wouldn't exist without Parker's, would it? Poor Frank. His wife keeps him straight when she's not off fucking everything in trousers.'

He seemed to be wandering. I didn't dare to look at Marcie to see how she was taking this. Just in case Frank misinterpreted the movement.

'It's your fault,' he said.

For a moment I thought he meant me, but he was looking at Parker.

'Me?'

Parker looked astonished.

'You. If you'd been half the man your dad was. You know what he did to your daughter, little Kim, and my sister.'

Suddenly he shot his free hand out at Marcie. She flinched. Frank laughed.

'Doesn't matter about her. Doesn't matter, good old Marcie. But Kim. You never did a fuck, did you? You just took it. That was the last straw. It was up to me. It takes a man. He never guessed I was waiting for the chance to get him.'

'Frank,' Marcie moaned, but I had the feeling she wasn't conscious of having spoken.

'Pathetic,' Frank shouted at the top of his voice. Then he did it again.

'Pathetic. That's what he called me. None of them noticed I'd gone. Too busy touching up Marcie. He says to me. He says "Frank, let's have a talk." He says he wants me to be a witness. He says my wife's a whore and my brother-in-law treats me like shit. Why don't I inform on them. Turn informer. Your dad would have pissed on him. It takes a man.'

The gun moved as if he was about to demonstrate.

'Is that when it happened? The accident.'

Feeble, but I had to say something, and I didn't fancy using words like kill at that precise moment.

He laughed like a man remembering a funny incident.

'There was a knife in the back seat. Just lying there. I couldn't believe it. Mr Councillor bleeding Edwards, carrying a knife. But you're all the same. He never saw me picking it up. He wasn't even looking at me. What about your wife I says, the dirty bitch, and he turns round and slaps me. So I stuck him and walked away.'

If only, I thought. If only Aston hadn't put the knife he'd taken away from Tony in the car. If only Tony hadn't had it in the first place. If only.

'Did you know?' I asked Marcie.

She shook her head. She looked white and ill, as if she could hardly stand up. She swayed and Parker put his arm round her. Frank tottered on his feet, and then recovered himself, as if Marcie's unsteadiness had been contagious.

'That's right,' he said. 'Biddies. I don't trust you biddies over the water. At all. At all.'

He laughed.

'What about Walter?'

It was a toss-up whether he'd collapse or pull the trigger, but I wouldn't have liked to bet on it.

'Oh, Walter. A cunning little bastard. That was his Welsh blood. Aston told him all about Miller. So he rings them up. He wants the nomination. Wants to be the MP. That monkey.'

He didn't tell us what Parker's dad would have done but I could imagine. And Walter was using me, either to put pressure on Parker and Marcie or perhaps to double cross them and bring things out into the open without being involved himself. Either way, I'd been had. Again.

'What are we going to do about Walter?' Frank said.

It was a passable imitation of Marcie.

'They never asked me,' he went on. 'I rang him up and told him Marcie wanted to see him on the estate. I banged him on the head and dumped him out the window. Easy.'

He swayed again and recovered himself, stood up straight,

wiped his mouth and flexed his shoulders.

'You two.' He gestured with the gun. 'Outside. Hands behind your head.'

We did what he said and he backed slowly out of the passageway in front of us. I was waiting for him to stumble on the doorstep but he didn't, and he'd moved a couple of steps out to the very edge of the square of light from the open door when the front window banged open and Marcie's voice screamed at him.

'Frank. Don't.'

He stumbled then, and I reached him before Aubrey. Afterwards I told him that it was because I was nearest, but I think the truth is that I was a lot more frightened and the terror lent my feet wings.

I hit him square on with my whole body. The shotgun went off with a roar as we hit the floor. I wrestled it away from him with surprising ease, but I was in the middle of a white hot burning flash of fear and rage that had gone off as I jumped at him, and right there under me was the man who had killed Aston and Walter and I hit him with the shotgun and hit him again, feeling the blows going in with that wet soft thudding sound until I felt Aubrey and Parker holding me and pulling me back away from him. I struggled for a bit to get back and hit him again but in a moment I realised that he wasn't moving any more.

Marcie went past me and threw herself down beside him. She lifted his head into her lap. He was bleeding from a cut in his forehead and his lips looked smashed and swollen.

'Get an ambulance,' she shouted at Parker. 'The site office.'

Parker hesitated.

'What about — ?'

He gestured with his open hands as if he didn't quite know what he wanted to say.

'Don't be stupid,' Marcie said venomously. 'Get an ambulance.'

Chapter 34

In the early hours of the morning I was sitting in the interview room at the police station. They hadn't handcuffed me and the desk sergeant had looked a little bit surprised when they brought me in, but of course he had an image to sustain, so he managed to process me as if he'd never seen me before or showed me up to Borelli's room.

Borelli himself came down and took my statement later on. I hadn't killed Frank as I'd feared at first. Parker was somewhere else in the station making his statement and Marcie was at the hospital with Frank.

Borelli believed me, but he wasn't happy about it, and when I gave him the edited highlights of my activities over the last few days he flew into a rage. In the end he softened up a bit and told me that he was letting Tony go, and that if I hadn't obstructed justice by keeping quiet about what was going on, the boy might have been free days ago.

I'd had a good laugh at the idea of Borelli defending justice, and that's probably why he'd kept me sitting there, instead of letting me go home. But I wasn't too worried about that. They'd let Aubrey go after they'd questioned him and I guessed that he'd have roused one of the solicitors I knew. It would probably be someone who I'd rung up in the past to come and get him out.

I'd have laughed again, except I didn't feel like laughing. Somehow the worst thing was that what Frank had done had been a sort of accident. Nothing to do with Aston's work or what he believed, merely what he stood for in Frank's fuddled mind. If the man had been thirty years younger he'd probably be standing on the football terraces with his mates, shouting 'Kill the nigger' every time a black player touched the ball. That was how it was, and Frank had simply been an outlet for a current that ran through the group in which he had grown up and lived.

He'd known the way that old Parker would have dealt with Aston, and he'd found out that Keith didn't have the power or the courage, so he'd demonstrated his manhood in the only way he knew how.

I kept thinking about how I'd wanted to smash him, to obliterate him, end his life: and I knew that it wasn't just because of Aston or Walter. While I was hitting him he'd been the other, my enemy, the source of my troubles.

The odd thing was that, before I knew what he'd done, something about his eyes had occasionally reminded me of Shelagh, and I'd been disposed to like him for that reason. But that feeling had vanished when I leapt at him, even though I'd known all the time that he was just a poor drunken slob, whose identity only survived in the idea of himself as the enemy of people like me, and I hated the way my moment of blind and passionate fury had echoed his. As for Shelagh; that was the sort of contradiction I was used to living with.

I wondered what Aston would have thought, because I was sure that in my place he'd have done the same. But when I thought of him I thought about when we were children and the long time before I'd seen him again, and I thought about how he'd got killed just when he was going to get what he wanted, he was going to defeat history at last, and I thought that it was nothing really, no big tragedy, because we'd come from people who'd always had to exist in this driven way, so we could survive whatever happened, even the way we had to live and die in this beautiful and hard-faced city, and just when I thought

I had it in proportion, that I understood it all, I felt something give inside me and just in time I turned my back on the watchful eyes of the policeman standing in the corner, put my hand in front of my face and struggled to control my tears. Then I thought oh bugger it, who gives a shit what this little twerp thinks, but by then the moment had gone.

UNIVERSITY OF ST. THOMAS LIBRARIES

PR 6066 .H485 L38 1990
Phillips, Mike, 1941-
The late candidate

WITHDRAWN
UST
Libraries